WAITING *for* HEAVEN

Stories and Poems that
Inspire Faith, Hope and Trust

ROB K SIMMONS

Waiting for Heaven
Copyright © 2021 by Rob K Simmons

All rights reserved. No part of this publication may be reproduced, distributed, or transmitted in any form or by any means, including photocopying, recording, or other electronic or mechanical methods, without the prior written permission of the author, except in the case of brief quotations embodied in critical reviews and certain other non-commercial uses permitted by copyright law.

Sketch Artist: Rebekah Lay

Tellwell Talent
www.tellwell.ca

ISBN
978-0-2288-7149-1 (Hardcover)
978-0-2288-6683-1 (Paperback)
978-0-2288-7150-7 (eBook)

FOREWORD

It gives me great pleasure to introduce you to Rob Simmons and his collection of short stories and poems. Rob had been creating and compiling the following ideas over a period of years. I hope that you find them as inspirational as I have.

They all have an underlying theme in them, and that is to trust; a trust that will help you in your everyday tasks.

Paul Banks

**BIBLE STORIES FROM
GRANDDAD STORIES 1**

WORSHIP

"Hi Granddad. We've been trying to share our faith with kids at school, but some are saying that we don't have to worship God now. Isn't it enough to know that Jesus is our Friend?" Louise wanted to know.

"It is great that you know Jesus as your Friend, but worship is still really important."

"Why," asked **Remington.**

"Turn with me to Luke 4:8. After Jesus had spent 40 days in the wilderness, Satan tempted Jesus to worship him. Satan promised Jesus that he would give Him everything in the world if He did that. What Jesus said was very interesting. He said, 'You shall worship the Lord, your God, and **Him only shall you serve.** Worship involves service. Everyone worships something, no matter what they believe; even atheists. Whatever they worship, they serve in some way."

"Really? Atheists don't even believe in God. Who or what do they worship?" **Louise** was quite surprised at that statement.

"We worship God through prayer and Bible Study and by trying our best to live the way God wants us to live. That could include helping people with food if they're hungry, or just talking with them; listening to their story. You would be amazed how much good just listening to someone can do. When you understand their situation, you can help them to see how Jesus is the answer to their problems and situations. Atheist also share what they believe by telling people that God is not real. They say that we should get as much as we can out of this life because there is nothing else to come. Atheists have different moral values and beliefs to what we do. For them, if it feels good, do it. The down side to that is, someone usually ends up getting hurt or discouraged. Some people decide that this life is a nightmare and end their own life. In atheism there is no hope for anything better, because we got here by accident and there's nothing better to come."

Remington wanted to know, "You said that everyone worships something. How are we to know what other people worship?

"Here's how you can tell what people worship. Where does their time and money go? Who, or what are they most interested in? You see, worship involves time and money. As Christians we are focused on loving Jesus and spreading the Gospel of the Kingdom and His soon return. We pay tithes and offerings to help spread the Gospel. We attend church regularly. People worship many things. If their worship is not directed higher than themselves it will be directed lower. Even today people worship statues or animals, like cows. If they worship nothing else, they will worship themselves."

"How do people worship themselves?" **Louise** wanted to know.

"Some people spend a lot of time thinking about themselves. They will spend a lot of money on makeup and clothes and shoes to look as beautiful as they can so that people will praise them and tell them how wonderful they look. The

Bible calls this vanity. Others buy expensive cars or large houses so that they look like they are successful, even if they are greatly in debt by so doing. The important thing for them is that people admire them and treat them like someone really important. Whatever your time and money is spent on; whatever has the most of your attention and efforts; that is your idol."

"I know what you mean Granddad. I know some kids who are into my little ponies or comic books so much that they spend lots of money buying the stuff and all their time is spent on things related to what they love." **Remington** thought that they were crazy.

"Yes, and some people are mad about sports, attending all of the games being played by their favourite team and spending lots of money on tickets and travel etc. People love it when you can share their excitement and interest in whatever they are into. With some people, if you don't share in their excitement they can turn nasty. That happened to Paul. When he was in Ephesus, he was very successful in turning people to Christ. Some people who worshipped the goddess Dianna got upset because people stopped worshipping her. It wasn't long before people became angry and started shouting out, 'Great is Dianna of the Ephesians.' [Acts 19:28.] They went to the officials to try to have Paul stoned. You see how persecution works? Whenever someone accepts Jesus they leave something else. People then get upset because the one who accepts Jesus changes for the better. That is a slap in the face for those who don't change, because their own sin and selfishness is exposed."

"Is that why some people don't want to know us? They think we're weird." observed **Louise.**

"Probably. The thing about worshipping God is, it always makes you a better person for it. You can learn so many skills that you didn't have, I know I did. As you do what you can to help other people you gain leadership skills, compassion, sympathy, teaching, study techniques, all the fruits of the Spirit, such as love, joy, peace, patience etc. The point is you always are better off with God. Our faith is love based. God wants only the best for us. He is worthy of our worship and devotion. Just look what Jesus did for us. He loved us so much that He died a horrible death in our place so that we wouldn't have to. Because He died and rose back to life again, we can be sure that He is able to give us eternal life as well."

"What about people who don't worship Jesus? What are their lives like?" **Remington** asked.

"Children, this world is in a mess. Without the guidance that God gives in the Bible, people are left to figure out for themselves how best to live, and what their code of behavior will be. [Rom. 10:3.] Even the most law-abiding people fall into traps that hurt them. Here, drinking alcohol is thought to be a very good thing to do. People spend a lot of money on this habit. Often going to the pub is more important to them than buying food or paying bills. Alcohol such as beer or wine becomes an idol worshipped by many. There are other vices that I won't go into here. Many fall into the trap of lust that degrades and cheapens a beautiful gift that our Creator gave to us before sin entered the world; the gift of intimacy. One thing I do know; those who worship God are Christ centered and look for opportunities to help others. Most other people are self-centered, caring mainly for what they want."

"So, if sport and hobbies and drink etc. can be idols which are bad for us, how can we know if something we like and want to be involved in is OK?" **Louise** was getting frustrated.

"You love Jesus, right? Anything that you want to do that you would feel happy inviting Jesus along as well is OK. If you think Jesus wouldn't like it, then don't do it. Also, is what you want to do going to help someone else? If playing a sport or some other activity will help someone else find Jesus, do it. My point is, guard against selfishness. Always look for ways to serve Jesus and help others to find Him. It all comes down to motive."

"I think I need to pray about this Granddad." **Remington** suggested.

"Great idea. Prayer is us chatting with Jesus. He answers us through the Bible, through church, and sometimes through friends. The Holy Spirit will give you peace with the answer if it is from God. Also, the way will open up for you to do what God wants you to do. Does that answer your question children? Remember, God alone is worthy of worship and you will always be better off if you worship Him."

"Thanks Granddad. We knew we could count on you to explain it to us." Smiled **Louise.**

"Goodbye children. God bless."

GRANDDAD STORIES 2

JESUS

"Granddad, you told us that we need to get to know Jesus personally, not just know about Him in order to live a good life now and to prepare for the future life. Who is Jesus really Granddad?" **Remington** wanted to know.

"First of all Jesus is on your side. He wants to be your Friend. Jesus said in John 15:14 that you are His friends if you are willing to do what He wants. To show just how good a Friend He is, in verse 13 He tells us that the greatest act of love a person can do is for someone to die for his friends. That's exactly what Jesus did. [Phil. 2:8.] He died for you two, and me too of course. Then He rose from the grave to show that death has no power over Him, and that He has the power to save us from death. Now we can choose to live for Him."

"If Jesus wants us to obey Him, how hard will it be to do what He wants?" asked **Louise.** She really didn't like hard work.

"Let's ask our Friend Jesus. He invites us in Matt. 11:28-30 to come to Him with all our burdens and problems and He will give us rest. Then we will learn from Him how to obey Him. Do you know what will happen if we do that? In John 15:11 Jesus says that we will be filled with His **JOY.** So what does He want us to do? Verse 12, He wants us to love one another and share the love of Jesus with as many people as we can. Now, is that too hard, is it?"

"Does that mean I have to love her?" complained **Remington,** referring to his sister.

"Afraid so. Jesus has already done most of the hard work. He just wants us to help him out a little. He wants us to trust Him. In fact He said that if we have faith, even as little as a grain of mustard seed, we'll be able to move mountains. [Matt. 17:20.] Isn't that something? That means that we'd be able to do heaps more things than we ever thought we could."

"One thing that I love about Jesus is the way He used to tell stories to help even humble people to understand important truths. Stories like the good Samaritan. [Luke 10:33,34.] Here a total foreigner and an enemy to Israel sees a Jewish man wounded badly and he looks after him, even when his own people have ignored his needs. It shows that all men are our brothers and should be treated kindly. Jesus told many stories, all with good messages. Another thing I love is the way He treated people. The woman at the well was a Samaritan who was shunned, even by her own people. Jesus talked with her and accepted her and told her that He was the Messaiah. She became a really good disciple." [John 4:7-30.] Do you think Jesus is powerful enough to look after you? If so, why?"

Remington answered, "Yes! He's more powerful than Superman."

"Let's check that out. Baby Superman came from Krypton, a doomed planet, to Earth, a planet with a yellow sun which gave the baby great powers. Jesus, Who is God in Heaven, by the word of His mouth created all the worlds, stars and suns that exist. [Hebrews 1:8,10.] I think Jesus wins that round. What about Aquaman? He can swim fast in water. Jesus can walk on water. [Matt. 14:25.] What about Thor, the god of thunder who can create storms? Jesus can calm the storms. [Luke 8:25.] I could go on about other supposed comic heroes, but they are all make believe, they're not real. Jesus is real. He can, and does, do far more for you than a comic hero could do, even if they were real."

"Like what Granddad?" **Louise** wanted to know.

"Like Jesus turned water into grape juice, unfermented wine. [John 2:8-10.] He also fed thousands of people with just a few barley loaves and some small fish. [Luke 9:16,17.]

Sound like a good Friend to have? He healed people of all manner of diseases, including demon possession, mental problems, palsy, leperacy, blindness, people unable to talk and many others. He preached the Gospel and taught in their synagogues." [Matt.4:23,24.]

"Wow Granddad, that's much better than Superman." exclaimed **Remington.**

"Yes, and He's given us far more than that. When He could no longer be here in person He sent the Holy Spirit to teach us, protect us, encourage us and more. The Spirit also gives us gifts. He gives us the armour we need to overcome the devil. That armour is truth, righteousness, the Gospel of peace, faith, salvation and most of all, the Sword of the Spirit, which is the Word of God, the Bible. He also gives us other gifts such as the ability to preach, teach, prophesy, heal, be generous, speak in toungues etc. He also gives us fruit......"

"Like apples and oranges and mangoes?" interjects **Remington.**

"No Rem. Like love, joy, peace, patience, gentleness, goodness, faith, meekness and temperance. [Gal. 5:22,23.] As you love and serve Jesus your character changes and you begin to love others as Jesus loves, you become more patient and filled with joy and peace etc."

"Granddad, what about God the Father? He seems pretty stern and hard to please." enquired **Louise.**

"Not at all. Jesus was asked by Philip, one of His disciples, to show them the Father. Jesus said that the Father is just like He is, and that He and the Father are one. [John 14:8,9.] The Father is also our Saviour. [1 Timothy 1:1.] God loves us and wants to save us because God **IS** love." [1 John 4:8.]

"You know what I like best about Jesus? He loved children. [Matt. 19:13-15.] People who enter the Kingdom of Heaven must learn to trust Jesus just as a little child trusts his loving father. In that way they become obedient and child like; not childish but childlike. My greatest wish is to let go of what I want to do and be willing to do what Jesus, my best Friend wants. I know Jesus is also my Saviour and my King and my God, therefore I should respect and worship Him, and I do. But most of all He is my **FRIEND**, not because I chose Him but because He chose me to be His friend. [John 15:16.] He has invited me to share His love with as many people as I can so that they also may have the chance to become His friend. It is my greatest pleasure to do so."

"I want to be His friend too Granddad." said **Louise.** "So do I." chimed in **Remington.**

"That's easy. Next time you talk to Jesus, just ask Him to come into your heart and be your Friend, and He will.

When you sin, ask Him to forgive you, and He will. Share what Jesus means to you with others and you will have a joy that you have never known before. You won't have to worry about your place in Heaven. Jesus, your Friend has already booked that for you. When you're not sure what the best or right thing to do is, just ask yourself, 'what would Jesus do?' then do it."

"**Louise** said, "Let's pray now Granddad.""

"We all knelt down and **Louise** prayed a simple, little prayer."

"Dear God, I want Jesus to come into my life today and be my friend. I choose to follow Him as well as I can from now on. Thank you Father, in Jesus' name, amen." We said amen and we all had tears rolling down our cheeks for happiness."

"God bless you children."

GRANDDAD STORIES 3

CREATION

"Granddad, the teacher at school told us that there is no God, and that we are here because we evolved from other animals. That didn't sound right. Can you help us?" asked **Louise.**

"That's a very big question and an important one. I will do my best to answer but it may take some time."

"In the beginning God did something very beautiful. He created a perfect world; made 2 perfect people and placed them in a perfect garden. Gen. 1:26 - 31. They had all the food that they could possibly want to eat to keep them healthy and happy. Gen. 1:29. The Record tells us that God gave them the freedom to choose to love and obey Him or to rebel. The only test they had was to stay away from the Tree of Knowledge of Good and Evil, which was right in the middle of the garden. They were told to stay together and warned that if they ate of its fruit they would surely die. They chose to disobey and they ate some of the fruit. Gen 3:6. As sin always does their actions brought immediate results. The worst was that they lost their innocence and they were immediately driven from the garden. They could no longer enjoy the same close connection that they used to have with God. Sin separates."

Remington said, "that's sad Granddad."

"Yes, but God didn't leave them without hope. He promised that one day a Deliverer would come, defeat God's enemy and make it possible for them to have a sinless life once again. They were permitted to live for hundreds of years before the penalty of death claimed them. During that time God gave them many precious gifts to help them live this life and to prepare for the next life. From sinless Eden came marriage and the Sabbath. They had guardian angels to guide and protect them [Matt. 18.10.] and the Holy Spirit to teach and convict them to do right. They had children, many of whom rebelled against God. Their sins became so bad that God had to destroy everything except Noah and his family in a worldwide flood. After the flood the people multiplied. Eventually Jesus was born. He came to show them just how much the Father loved them. He gave His life to pay for their sins and made it possible for them to have a home in the perfect Paradise of God forever."

"But Granddad, what has all that got to do with evolution?" **Louise** seemed confused.

"Here is a real truth that you can trust. **For every beautiful gift God gives us for our well being, Satan has a counterfeit to mislead and destroy Gods people.**"

"Now for evolution. Let's compare what evolution says to what the Bible says and you will see the difference. The Bible says that we were created by an eternal, loving, all powerful, all knowing and ever present God. Because of that **we are answerable to Him** for the choices that we make, to obey Him or not."

"Evolutionists say that many millions of years ago some mysterious gasses appeared out of nowhere and exploded. Somehow after the explosion, these gasses became matter which was hurled far away. One piece of matter became the sun. Others, when they cooled, became planets and moons and asteroids etc. They say that on planet Earth certain enzymes came together in a primeval ooze to become simple life forms. These life forms multiplied and over millions of years changed, evolved, into all the different kinds of life forms we now have on Earth. These enzymes became fish which became animals and birds and bugs. They say that people came from monkeys. Can you believe that children? Evolutionists say that there is no God, that we got here by accident. Therefore there was no original sin which means that there is nothing for Jesus to save us from. Jesus means nothing to them but a swear word. They say that **we don't have to answer to anyone. We are free to live and act however we like. There is no judgement and no eternal life hereafter."**

Louise wanted to know, "what's the point of living if there is nothing better to look forward to?"

"The Bible says we are getting weaker and weaker the further we get from Creation. Our bodies and minds are nowhere near as good or big or strong or healthy as were the bodies and minds of Adam and Eve."

"Evolutionists say we are evolving and getting better and better with each change. I wonder what man is supposed to evolve into next? Satan said to Eve that if she ate the fruit we will be like Gods knowing good and evil, and that we will never die. I haven't seen that happen yet except that we have an ever increasing knowledge of evil."

We cannot scientifically prove that there is a God but neither can those who deny Him, called atheists, prove that there isn't a God. All we can do is look at the evidence on both sides and decide for ourselves what to believe. It takes faith to believe that a loving God created everything. That faith is based on evidence. I can show from archaeology, mathematics, history and Bible prophecy that the Bible is true and trustworthy. It never changes. God is just who He said He was."

"What evidence do evolutionists have for their beliefs Granddad?" asked **Remington.**

"It takes faith to believe in evolution. There is no proof of gasses exploding. One type of animal cannot mate with another type of animal outside its family grouping and produce a viable offspring. God said at creation that each kind of animal must reproduce **after its own kind. Gen. 1:24.** You can't have a lion and a dear mating and producing offspring for example. It can never happen, thus showing evolution to be false. They claim that fossils found in rock strata, showing simple forms of life low down and more advanced lifeforms higher up proves that as time went on simple animals evolved into more complex animals. The flood of Noah's time answers that challenge. As the waters rose higher more advanced animals were able to get to higher ground."

Carbon 14 dating is another evidence evolutionists use to prove their case. This measures the amount of carbon in rocks etc. The lower the carbon level the older the rocks. By this means they date objects back millions of years. Unfortunately for them the carbon level in rocks and other objects runs out after 10,000 years. Their evidence is false."

"So how can we be sure that Creation is right Granddad?" **Louise** wanted to know.

"Archaeology is one way. Skeptics used to poke fun at Christians for believing that the Hittite nation existed as there was no mention of it anywhere outside Scripture. "Only in the Bible" they would say until the Rosetta stone was discovered. It had 3 languages on it. 2 were known languages, the third was the Hittite language, thus proving the Bible to be true."

"Another way is through time prophecy. The Bible predicts events hundreds of years in advance. These events are specific and often the exact time is given for their fulfillment. The prophecies always come true. The birth, life, death and resurrection of Jesus are excellent examples. Read Isa. 53. It's all about Jesus."

There is much more evidence, but this will do for now. **The real question is, which one do you choose children, evolution or Creation?** Choose Creation and you are shown how to live this life in as happy a way as you can and have the hope of eternity with Jesus. Choose evolution and you are born, you live and decide for yourself what you do with all the consequences that comes from your choices without guidance from a loving God, then you die. There is no eternity for you. As for me, I choose Jesus."

"So do we Granddad. Now we know that the teacher is not right in this subject."

"God bless you children. What will we study next time?"

Granddad Rob.

GRANDDAD STORIES 4

SACRIFICES

"Granddad, how could He? How could God tell Israel to kill all those innocent animals? How cruel?" **Louise** was upset.

Louise and Remington were visiting granddad for the school holidays. Granddad was reading through the Bible with them for worship when they came to the story of animals being sacrificed as a sin offering to God, and it horrified the kids.

"There is a very good reason for it children. Would you like to hear a story? I think it will explain all the blood and gore."

"Ok, but I still think it's cruel." complained **Louise**.

"A long time ago, before the world was created, God had made beautiful beings we call Angels. Their greatest delight was to praise God in song and in worship. They didn't have to, they wanted to. They carried messages from God all over the universe. The greatest angel, the leader of the Heavenly choir was named Lucifer. He truly loved God with all his heart until one day he became jealous. He accused God of being unfair by expecting angels to obey His will and His rules. [Eze. 28:13,14.] He led a rebellion of a third of all the angels. Eventually there was war in Heaven and Lucifer, meaning Day Star, [Isa. 14:12.] became Satan the rebel. What made him so jealous was that the Godhead was planning the creation of the Earth and he was not involved. When God created the Earth in all its perfection and beauty it drove Satan mad. Adam and Eve were created, our first parents. Satan lost the war in Heaven and was cast out into outer darkness. [Rev. 12:7-9.]

"He chose to come to Earth to ruin God's new creation. God let him stay. Adam and Eve were warned about him and were told to stay together and to stay away from that tree; don't eat its fruit, don't touch it, don't look at it, just stay away from it. God told Adam that to eat the fruit of that tree was to die. [Gen. 2:16,17.]

"But Granddad, what has that got to do with all those poor animals being slaughtered?" **Remington** wanted to know.

"I'm coming to that. One day Eve wandered away from Adam and before she knew it, she was right in the middle of the garden where the forbidden tree was. Did she get scared and run away from there? No! She looked longingly at the tree and its fruit and as she did, she heard a voice coming from the tree. It was the serpent, the loveliest creature in the garden. It told Eve that it was ok to eat the fruit, that God didn't really mean what He said. So, she believed the serpents lie and ate the fruit. When Adam came along, he was horrified at what he saw but he also ate the fruit so he could die with his wife." [Gen 3:1-6.]

"Here is the really important point. When Adam and Eve ate that fruit, they disobeyed God. Disobedience to God is sin. Really, they committed treason against their King and obeyed the enemy, Satan; in the form of a serpent in the garden. Their action demanded the death penalty. The Bible says the wages of sin is death. [Rom. 3:23.]

God told them they would die if they ate the fruit, and they would have if God hadn't done something very special. God Himself took an innocent lamb, killed it, thus making atonement for the sins of Adam and Eve and used the skin of the lamb to make clothes for the couple. In their innocence they were clothed in a garment of light, but when they sinned that light disappeared. They were left exposed, naked. They tried to hide their shame behind fig leaves but we can never hide our sins that way. If that lamb hadn't died Adam and Eve would have. The lamb took their place. Gen. 3:7,21."

"But Granddad, it still seems so unfair. The lamb did nothing wrong." **Louise** was still not happy.

"That is true. The lamb was completely innocent. It was part of God's master plan to rescue the human race from the penalty that sin would bring on them, death and destruction. You see, there were only 2 choices. Either the sinful race could die in their sins forever separated from God or God Himself could pay for their sins by dying in their behalf. All the lambs and all the goats and all the bulls that were killed for the sins of the people all pointed forward to what God was going to do to fix the sin problem forever."

"But how can poor animals dying help the sin problem?" Enquired **Remington**.

"God knew that we couldn't save ourselves so He made a way for man to be free of sin if he trusted in the promise of God. The animals that died were only a temporary fix. God Himself became a man and lived among us yet without sin. He taught us how to lead a better life and how to trust in God and how to love Him. The Bible is very clear that Jesus, the Son of God was the Lamb slain from the foundation of the world. [Rev. 13:8.] Only Jesus could completely pay for our sins because only Jesus was worth more than all of us put together. His shed blood paid for all of the sins of all mankind for all time. If we sin now all we have to do is to ask His forgiveness, trusting by faith that He will forgive us and give us the will to obey in future. [1 Jn. 1:9]. All the animals that ever died pointed forward to Jesus Who died so that we may live."

"Granddad, it's getting worse. First all those animals had to die and now Jesus died too? Why?" **Louise** spoke for both children.

Sin is deadly. It always involves a cost. Adam and Eve were driven out of the Garden of Eden and had to watch as the plants, animals and even their own children died or rebel against God and become savage. Sin cost the lives of all those animals. Sin cost the life of the Son of God. [Phil. 2:5-10.] We don't have to kill animals now to pay for our sins. All we have to do is to confess our sins to Jesus and forsake them, but every time we sin, we break the heart of God because we are saying that we reject His sacrifice for us, and we don't love Him enough to obey Him. He only asks us to do what will protect us and make us happy. God loved us enough to die for us. [Jn. 3:16-18.] Do you love Him enough to live for Him?"

With tears running down their faces the children promised that they would try from then on to live for Jesus.

"We still don't like it but now we see that it was sin that caused the death of all those animals. God wasn't being horrible, sin was. Thanks for helping us understand Granddad." **Louise** was so grateful now.

"You're welcome children. Come back again and we will see if we can understand a little better what the Bible is telling us next time."

9/1/21.

GRANDDAD STORIES 5

SALVATION

"Hi children, welcome. What's up Lulu? You looking troubled."

"Oh Granddad," complained **Louise**, "every time I try to do good and obey God I muck it up and end up doing the opposite. I want to obey God but the harder I try the worse I get. I don't know what to do."

I know exactly what you mean. I used to have that problem. I found the Sabbath especially hard to keep. As you know, it is the 4th commandment, found in Exodus 20:8-11. Do you remember how verse 8 begins?"

Remington quoted, "Remember the Sabbath day to keep it Holy."

"That's right Remington, but how do you keep it holy? All I knew was that I couldn't do this or I couldn't do that. In Isa. 58:13 it tells me that I was not even allowed to speak my own words or think my own thoughts. It got really hard to control my thoughts and actions all day. Going to church was easy, but even then I became critical of people who were not observing Sabbath the way I thought it should be kept. I was a mess."

"But Granddad, people say that we don't have to keep the Sabbath now. They say we are not under law now but under grace. Is that right?" asked **Louise.**

"We **are** under grace, but that makes it more important to obey God. In Matt. 5:17-19 Jesus makes it quite clear that He didn't come to do away with the law, and that it will remain until all is fulfilled. James tells us that to break one commandment is to break them all. He also says that we will be judged by the "law of liberty." James 2:8-12. Rev. 12:17 tells us that God's people will keep the commandments of God and have the Testimony of Jesus, which is the Holy Spirit Who is the Spirit of prophecy. Isaiah reveals that in Heaven we will be worshipping God from one Sabbath to another Sabbath. There is no doubt in my mind that Sabbath, and the law, are still very important to God, even now."

"But why is the Sabbath so important Granddad?" **Remington** wanted to know.

"Way back at Creation, God rested on the Seventh day and made it holy. Gen. 2:2, 3. It is a memorial that God was indeed the One who made everything, and that we didn't evolve from other life forms or get here in some other way. He, God, made us. We are His by Creation. Exodus 20:11 makes that very clear. After Moses told us how to keep the Sabbath he told us why. God created everything in 6 days and rested on the 7th day and made it holy. The Sabbath is the Seal of God in that it reveals who He is; the Lord, what He did; created or made; the territory over which He has dominion; the heavens and the Earth. We know Saturday is the 7th day Sabbath because the Jews have kept the same day all through their generations as it was given to them by God. No one has the right to change what God has established. We know it is a literal 24 hour day and not a thousand years, because the Hebrew word used for day in the creation account is "YOM!" Whenever this word has a number in front of it, it is always a 24 hour day. In Hebrews 4:4, 9 Paul tells us that God rested from His creation works on the Sabbath. Further he says that there remains a keeping of the Sabbath for the people of God. That would be a silly argument if creation was just a story. Paul took it very literally. Jesus also took creation very literally too. Look in Matt. 19:4. Answering a question on divorce He quotes creation as His argument against divorce. That would make no sense if there was no literal creation. It shows that you either believe all the Bible or you don't. You can't pick and choose what you believe."

"But Granddad, you still haven't answered my question." complained **Louise.** "How can I be good when all I do ends up bad?"

"There is an old expression, 'what gets your attention gets you.' Because you are always thinking about your behaviour and what you do wrong, your faults get burned deeper and deeper into your mind. It becomes very difficult to change for the better. Even if you do get better in one area you are at risk of becoming proud. You could think, 'I did it. I overcame that sin by my own efforts.' No children, there is a better way."

"What is it Granddad?" **Louise** wanted to know.

In John 15:12 Jesus gives us the answer. He says, 'If you **_LOVE_** me, keep My commandments. Don't you see? When you are focused on Jesus you become more and more like Him. If you want to be able to obey Jesus you have to get to know Him personally. You do that by talking to Him in prayer, by letting Him talk to you through His love letters to you, the Bible. Then you share with someone else how wonderful God is and invite them to get to know Jesus too. Going to church is great because you learn so much from the experiences of fellow believers and you gain new skills that you can use to serve God better."

"Then, what's the use of the commandments? Don't we have to keep them any more? asked **Remington**.

"That's a good question. When you truely love Jesus, you will no longer feel like you HAVE to keep the Commandments, you will WANT to keep them. THE Psalmist puts it this way; 'The law of the LORD is perfect, converting the soul. The commandment of the LORD is pure, enlightening the eyes. More to be desired are they than gold, yes, than much fine gold; sweeter also than honey and the honeycomb. [Psalm 19:7-10.] The 10 Commandments are like a mirror to point out to you all the dirt that is in your life. They are not soap, they can't make you clean. Only the blood of Jesus can do that. [Read Romans 8:1.] When you love Jesus, God doesn't see your sins, He sees only the blood of Jesus. Here's how it works; the more you love Jesus the more you want to please Him. You quickly lose interested in anything that He doesn't like. If you do sin, instead of having an animal killed to pay for your sin you go to Jesus directly in prayer, ask Him, the spotless Lamb of God, slain from the foundation of the world to forgive you. Do that and Jesus promised He will forgive you and forget your sin as if it never happened. [1 John 1:9.] Of course you have to decide in your heart that you never want to disappoint Jesus in that way again."

"Now children, can anyone tell me what sin is?"

"Sin is breaking the Law of God, doing something God doesn't want you to do or not doing what He does want you to do." answers **Louise**.

"Very good. Where did sin come from and who were the first sinners?"

"**Remington's** turn, "Adam and Eve sinned in the Garden of Eden." Gen. 3:6.

"Very true. If Creation was just a story then there was no First Sin. If there was no sin then there was no need for Jesus to die to pay for our sins. The Bible makes it clear right through that God is on a rescue mission to save us **from** sin, and to restore us to the perfection we had before sin began. Every page in the Bible tells us about Jesus and His love for us. God doesn't want to destroy people, He wants to get rid of sin. Sadly, most people still cling to their sins and will be destroyed along with them. It is their choice. That is why we must read and believe the Bible, to get to know and trust Jesus. Then we will have the power to live for Him."

"Remember how I said that I had trouble obeying God, especially on the Sabbath? Now that I am getting to know Jesus better I can understand more fully what those troublesome texts are really saying. Isaiah 58:13 says to not find your own pleasure or speak your own words on the Sabbath, but to call it a delight, the holy day of the Lord and honorable. Now I understand this text differently. What God is saying is, 'I love you. I want to spend time with you. I don't want anything else to distract you from spending time with Me.' If we do that then we will be greatly blessed by God because we have been able to spend a whole day with Him."

"Does that help you at all children?"

"Yeah Granddad, I think I understand now." replies **Louise**. "Instead of worrying about my behavior I need to get to know Jesus as my best Friend, then He will help me to obey."

"I think you have it children. God bless."

GRANDDAD STORIES 6

JOSEPH

"Lovely to see you 2 again. What would you like to hear about today?"

"Joseph!" answered **Remington.**

"Ok. Joseph had 11 brothers and 1 sister that we know of. He was the 2nd youngest. His dad had 4 wives but he loved Joseph's mum the best. Her name was Rachel. Joseph was the youngest son for a long time, the only son of his fathers favourite wife, and Jacob loved him more than all the others. Eventually his mother gave birth to a brother for Joseph named Benjamin. Sadly she died as soon as Benjamin was born."

"That's so sad Granddad." **Louise** said.

"Jacob was very upset for a long time, but worse was to come. The 10 older brothers were shepherds. They would take their sheep to wherever they could find enough pasture for their flocks to eat. As Joseph grew, Jacob would send him to find out how his brothers were doing. He would return to Jacob and give him a full report, good and bad. He thought that he was just obeying his dad, but several times the older brothers got into trouble because of Joseph's report. [Gen. 37:2.] This did not make him very popular with his half brothers, even though he only spoke the truth. Then God started giving Joseph dreams about his brothers bowing down to him. When Joseph told them the dreams it made the men furious. [Gen. 37:6-8.] They hated him as much as Jacob loved him. Jacob made Joseph a beautiful, new coat of many colours. [Gen.37:3,4.] The other brothers became so jealous of him that they wanted to get rid of him all together."

"That's terrible." cried **Remington.** "Louise annoys me sometimes but I still don't want to get rid of her." Louise gave him a shove.

"Their chance came when they were a long way from camp with their sheep. One day they saw Joseph coming over the hill wearing his pretty coat. They decided that this was their opportunity to get rid of him forever. They were going to kill him. The 4 oldest boys were Reuben, Simeon, Levi and Judah. When Reuben heard what they were planning he stopped them. Instead, he suggested throwing Joseph into a pit with the idea of rescuing him later. They stripped Joseph of his beautiful coat and threw him into a pit. Reuben went off to do something. While he was gone some Ishmaelite traders came near on camels, on their way to Egypt. Judah suggested that they sell Joseph to the Ishmaelites as a slave instead of killing him. They received 20 pieces of silver for him, a slaves price. [Gen. 37:26,27.] When Reuben returned he was furious. He had wanted to rescue Joseph out of the pit, but he was gone."

"What happened to Joseph next Granddad?" **Remington** wanted to know.

"First, let's see what the brothers got up to. After selling Joseph the brothers were feeling really guilty. Here is an important lesson to learn. **Sin has it's consequences.** Rarely does sin affect just the sinner. Usually more than one innocent person suffers because of that one, unconfessed sin. In this case the brothers killed a kid goat, dipped Joseph's beautiful coat in the blood of the goat, then returned home and lied to their father. They lead him to believe that some wild animal must have devoured Joseph in the wilderness. [Gen. 37:33.] The poor old man was beside himself with agony and pain, believing that his best loved son had been eaten and killed. For many days he was sobbing and no one could comfort him. The brothers had to watch as their beloved father lost all interest in life. They saw him mourn in deepest grief continually because of what they had done. Gen. 37:34,35.] Sin had it's consequences."

"But what happened to Joseph?" **Remington** repeated.

"The Ishmaelites sold Joseph to Potiphar, captain of the guards for Pharaoh, king of Egypt. Gen. [37:36] God blessed Joseph so much in Potiphar's service that soon he was running the whole property for his master. [Gen. 39:3,4.] Potiphar's wife desired to have Joseph, to get him to sin with her. [Gen. 39:7.] When Joseph refused to do what she wanted she lied to her husband, accusing Joseph of attacking her. [Gen. 39:17,18.] Potiphar threw Joseph into prison, even though he was innocent. [Gen. 39:20.] In prison God blessed Joseph so much for his faithfulness that soon he was running the whole prison. [Gen. 39:21,22.] The king's cup bearer and the kings baker were both in prison. Both had dreams and both told Joseph their dreams. God gave Joseph the meaning of their dreams. He told the cup bearer that in 3 days he would be released from jail to serve the pharaoh once again as he used to. He asked the cup bearer to mention him to pharaoh when he was released. [Gen.40:13,14.] The cup bearer promised he would but soon forgot his promise. In 3 days, according to his dream the baker was hanged and the birds ate his flesh. [Gen.40:19.]"

"So poor Joseph had to just rot in jail, is that right?" **Louise** wanted to know.

"I'm afraid so. Two more years Joseph spent in jail, then something incredible happened." [Gen. 41:1.]

"What happened Granddad?" **Remington** enquired.

"Pharaoh had a dream, in fact he had two dreams. In the first dream he saw 7 fat and healthy cows grazing by the river, then 7 skinny and sickly cows came along and ate up the fat cows, but they were no better off afterwards. The second dream was similar. 7 full, healthy stalks of wheat were happily growing when 7 skinny and blighted stalks came along and ate up the full plants but still remained skinny. [Gen. 41:2-7.] What dreams! What could it mean? All the magicians of Egypt couldn't give the king their meaning as hard as they tried. [Gen. 41:8.] Then the cup bearer remembered Joseph. Two years had passed since he promised Joseph to bring his case to Pharoh. [Gen 41:9-13.] When Joseph was called before Pharaoh out of prison he told Pharoh that the God that Joseph and his people worshipped had given him the answer to Pharaos dreams. [Gen.41:15,16.] He said that the 7 fat cows and the 7 full stalks of grain meant that for 7 years Egypt would have plenty of crops, far more than was needed. The 7 skinny cows and the 7 blighted stalks meant that the 7 years after that would be years of drought. [Gen. 41:28-31.] Joseph advised Pharaoh to find a wise man in his kingdom to be responsible for collecting 20% of all crops in the good years so that in the bad years the people would have something to eat. Pharaoh liked that idea and made Joseph his prime minister, second only to him." [Gen. 41:33:40.]

Louise asked, "did Joseph ever get to meet his brothers and father again?"

"Good question. I was just coming to that. When Joseph became prime minister, Pharaoh gave him a new name. It was **Zaphnathpaaneah**. It means 'one who reveals mysteries.' Wherever Joseph went, people were required to bow to him in reverence. [Gen. 41:43-45.] Joseph spoke like an Egyptian and dressed like an Egyptian, and now he had an Egyptian name. He was 30 years old when he became prime minister, about the same age as Jesus when He started His ministry." [Luke 3:23.]

"That's a hard name to pronounce. I think I'll just stick to Joseph." chuckled **Remington**.

"When the famine was at it's height Jacob sent Joseph's 10 brothers to Egypt to find grain to buy so that their families wouldn't starve. [Gen. 42:2.] When they met the Egyptian in charge of selling grain with a strange name of Zaphnathpaaneah they bowed themselves down to the ground before him. Joseph recognized his brothers and remembered his dream. [Gen. 42:6.] He remembered how his brothers treated him and how they sold him into slavery. There's another principle, **be sure your sins will find you out.** [Numbers 32:23.] This was his chance to get back at them, to make them pay for all the mean and horrible things they did to him. He had all the power now. He could kill them or enslave them if he wanted to........but he didn't."

"Why not, after all the rotten things that they did to him? **Louise** demanded.

"He still loved his brothers despite all the cruel things they did. Still, he wanted to test them. He wanted to see if they were still the evil men that they used to be. The brothers didn't recognize Joseph and Joseph closely questioned them as to where they came from and why they were there. He told them, 'you are spies, come to see the nakedness of the land.' [Gen. 42:9.] Joseph spoke through an interpreter in Egyptian. [Gen.42:23.] Eventually Joseph gave them grain but would not allow Simeon to return home with his brothers. He kept him in jail. [Gen. 42:24.] Simeon was a ring leader in wanting to kill Joseph and then in selling him into slavery. Joseph told the brothers that he would believe that they were not spies only if, when they returned to buy more grain they had their youngest brother, Benjamin with them. The brothers felt very bad for the way they had treated Joseph and lied to their father." [Gen. 40:21,22.]

"When they returned home and told Jacob all that had happened and the demand for Benjamin to go with them next time Jacob was furious and stubbornly refused to let him go. [Gen. 42:38.] After the grain was gone, Jacob had no choice. He had to send his sons back to Egypt to get more grain and he had to let Benjamin go with them, along with gifts for Joseph. [Gen. 43:11-13.] When they arrived back in Egypt Joseph saw Benjamin and was so happy, but he still didn't tell them who he was, not yet. He had more tests for them yet. Joseph put on a great feast for the brothers, including Simeon whom he had released from prison. Joseph arranged the brothers in age order at the table and gave them all good food, but to Benjamin he gave 5 times as much food as he did to anyone else. He wanted to see if they were still jealous men or if they really had changed." [Gen 43:33,34.]

"Joseph had one more test for the brothers. He secretly had his own personal goblet placed in Benjamins sack as the men were about to head home. As they were on their way Joseph sent soldiers to accuse the men of stealing, saying that the man in whos sack the goblet was found shall become a slave to Joseph, but the rest could go home. [Gen. 44:10.] The brothers believed that God was punishing them for what they did to Joseph. [Gen. 44:16.] Judah spoke to Joseph, explaining the conversation he had with his father concerning Benjamin. Judah asked if he could take Benjamins place and remain a slave so that his father wouldn't grieve himself to death over losing Benjamin also. [Gen.44:33,34.] Finally Joseph knew that his brothers were now good men. He burst into tears and told them, 'I am Joseph; is my father really alive still?' The brothers were terrified, except for Benjamin. [Gen. 45:3.] He told them to not worry for what they did to him because it was God Who sent Joseph to Egypt to preserve life." [Gen 45:4,5.]

"So did Joseph get to see his dad again?" asked **Louise.**

"Yes dear. Joseph sent the brothers home, all of them with as much grain as they could carry. He told them to tell their father that Joseph yet lives and is prime minister in Egypt. They were to tell him to come to Egypt to the land of Goshen so that Joseph could look after them for the remaining 5 years of famine. [Gen. 45:9-11.] At last Joseph got to hug his brother Benjamin and all his brothers. [Gen. 45:14,15.] Pharaoh heard of all that went on and he sent wagons back with the brothers to bring them all back to Egypt to live. Imagine how the brothers felt to tell Jacob that Joseph was still alive. It was more than Jacob could handle at first, but when he heard all that happened and saw the wagons from Egypt he agreed to go to Egypt with them. [Gen. 45:27,28.] Finally Joseph and his dad met and hugged and wept together a good while. Then Jacob was satisfied. [Gen. 46:29,30.] Jacob met Pharaoh and blessed him, then they all lived happily in the land of Goshen for the rest of their lives."

"Granddad, it seems to me that Joseph and Jesus are so similar." Observed **Louise.**

"How so?"

Louise continued, "He had step brothers who didn't believe in Him, [John 7:5] just as Joseph had trouble with his half brothers. After doing nothing but good for people for 3 1/2 years He was sold by Judas, one of His closest followers for 30 pieces of silver, a slaves price." [Matt.26:14,15.] Joseph was also sold for a slaves price by his brothers."

"Very good Lulu, you are right. There are many similarities between Joseph and Jesus. Here are some more. Although totally innocent, Joseph was imprisoned in a dungeon. Jesus also did nothing wrong but was crucified and spent days in the tomb." [John 19:41,42.]

"Just as the Jews and the Romans had to look on Him Whom they had pierced, [John 19:37.] so did the brothers of Joseph have to look on him whom they had betrayed."

"Joseph was sent by God to Egypt to save lives from the pestilence of famine. Jesus was sent by God to save humanity from the pestilence of sin." [Romans 6:23.]

"Just as Joseph brought to Egypt all His family to provide for them in a fertile land, so will Jesus bring with Him all who trust Him to His Fathers house, to a wonderful land where the redeemed shall live forevermore." [John 14:1-3.]

"We have also learned 3 very important lessons. What are they?"

Remington answered, "**be sure your sins will find you out.** You can't get away with anything. You'll eventually get caught."

Louise' turn, "**Sin has its consequences.** Your sins usually hurt someone else."

"That's right Lulu. Even if no one else knows what your sin is, it will still hurt someone. If no one else punishes you for your sins then you'll punish yourself. Whenever you sin you feel guilty. When you do it again you feel guilty again. You will keep punishing yourself until you confess it to Jesus and ask His forgiveness. If your sin involves someone else you must ask their forgiveness too. Then you can start to heal."

"The third lesson is, **God has a way to turn bad into good**. Even when your whole world seems to be falling apart as it did for Jesus on the cross when He cried out, 'My God, My God, why have you forsaken Me?' and for Joseph in prison, if we trust Him God is able to make good come from bad and blessings from cursings."

"Here's another lesson for parents, if you have more than one child, **don't play favourites.** If you do you could end up with a spoiled brat and much trouble in the household as Jacob found out."

"Children, God is calling you. He wants to bless you and use you to help many other people to find salvation just as he used Joseph to save lives. Jesus wants to come into your hearts and lives right now. Will you let Him?"

"Yes Granddad, we want that too." they both responded.

God bless children. See you next time.

GRANDDAD STORIES 7

AFTERLIFE

Louise was in tears as the children came in.

"What's wrong Lulu? Why are you crying?"

"A friend of mine from school died and I really miss her. Where is she now Granddad? What has happened to her?" **Louise** wanted to know.

"Where do you think she is?"

Remington was thoughtful. "Maybe her soul went to heaven after she died. That's what some people are saying. She was a good person after all and tried to live for Jesus."

"Let's see what the Bible says. What does Genesis 2:7 say?"

Louise read, "And the Lord God formed man of the dust of the ground, breathed into his nostrils the breath of life and man became a living soul."

"So what did God give Adam?"

"Body, breath and soul" answered **Louise.**

"Did He? Read it again."

Louise reread it and answered, "body, breath.... oh, I see. Man **BECAME** a living soul, he wasn't given a soul. **Body plus breath EQUALS soul.** So what happened to my friend after she died?"

"We'll get to that. Look at Genesis chapter 3:4,5. This is the first lie ever told the human family and so many people believe it today. God said eat the fruit and you will surely die. [2:17.] The devil said you will not surely die. [3:4.] When people believe that a loved one has gone to Heaven or hell or elsewhere they are believing the devil's lie."

"So what does happen when you die Granddad?" **Remington** wanted to know.

"Let's look at Ecclesiastes 12:7. At death our body return to the earth and become dust and our spirit, [Hebrew word ruach, meaning breath or wind] returns to God who gave it. It's interesting that the same Hebrew word for breath, [nephesh] applies to people and animals as well. In Ecc. 9:5 & 6 we are told that the dead know nothing and that even their emotions are gone. In verse 10 we are told to do all that we can while we live because in the grave there is no work nor device nor wisdom nor knowledge after death. I am glad of that because Heaven wouldn't be Heaven for me if I was there looking down at my loved ones on earth and seeing the daily struggles they go through and the stupid things they do or say that causes them so much pain."

"So no Heaven when we die, just a hole in the ground," suggests **Louise.** "That's pretty sad."

"Not really Lulu. We haven't finished yet."

"So what is death Granddad?" **Remington** wanted to know.

"Let's look at a few verses. Psalms 13:3. Here David suggests that death is sleep. Sleep is not so bad, is it? 1 Thess. 4:13-15. Here again Paul refers to death as a sleep. In John 11:11 Jesus told the disciples that their friend, Lazarus is asleep. The disciples thought, that's great, it means he is getting better. In verse 14 Jesus says plainly, 'Lazarus is dead.'"

"What about the soul? Doesn't that go to Heaven when we die?" asks **Louise.**

"Ezekiel tells us in chapter 18:4 That all souls belong to God and that the soul that sins shall die. Romans 3:23 says that all have sinned, therefore all deserve death. The good news is that the soul [person] who trusts in God doesn't have to die. Romans 6:23 says that the gift of God is eternal life through Jesus. When you understand that body plus breath equals soul it all makes sense. We don't **have** a soul, we **ARE** a soul."

"O.K. Granddad, we get it. We don't have a soul that goes to Heaven when we die, we are a soul. All we have to look forward to in death is a sleep where we know nothing and where we are buried in a hole in the ground. That's pretty depressing Granddad." **Louise** was starting to get impatient and upset again.

"Don't worry Lulu. It all gets better from here. Look at John 3:17 & 18. Jesus was sent to save the world, not to condemn it. Those who have accepted the Son of God have been promised life, not just here but forever. Besides, we can't take these corrupt, mortal bodies to Heaven with us. They wouldn't survive. God is going to give us new bodies. Everyone who is to be saved will get new bodies, whether they've been dead for 6,000 years or are still alive to meet Jesus when He comes. Look at 1 Corinthians 15:50-57. These verses tell us that we must be changed into an incorruptible form. That all happens when Jesus comes. Those sleeping in the graves will be brought to life and given immortal bodies and will live with Jesus forever, no more death ever. At least, that's what 1 Thessalonians 4:15-17 tells us."

"So after this body dies and rots, and the breath God gave me goes back to Him, what is there left of me that will make my new body me?" **Louise** thinks she has her old Granddad here.

"Your character. Every part of your life and even your thoughts are recorded faithfully in Heaven. [Rev. 20:12.]

When God gives you a new body He will restore your character and personality to that new body."

"That's really cool Granddad. That means that you'll get a new body too, hopefully one that is a lot younger and not so fat," said **Remington** with a smile on his face.

"You cheeky little monkey. I hope you're right too. No more aches and pains."

"Louise won't give up. "Doesn't the Bible say that when Jesus was on the cross he told the thief on the cross next to Him that the thief would be with Him in Paradise that day?" [Luke 23:43.]

"Did Jesus go to Paradise as soon as He died? If so, then why did He tell Mary to not touch Him on Sunday morning because He had not yet been to His Father? [John 20:17.] He rested on the Sabbath according to the commandment. All the punctuation in the Bible has been supplied by the interpreters as the original had no punctuation. Luke 23:43 should read, 'Truly, truly I tell you today, you shall be with me in Paradise.'"

"But what happens to people who are not saved? Do they burn forever?" **Remington** wanted to know.

"That is a good question Rem and the answer is in Revelation 20:4-6. There we see that the righteous live and reign with

Christ for 1,000 years after Jesus comes. By this time the New Jerusalem was back on the Earth made new. [Rev.21:1,2.] Satan and his demons have people to play with again because all the unsaved have been resurrected in the same condition as they were in when they went into their graves to receive their judgement. Because they had rejected Jesus they have to pay for their own sins in their own bodies. Even here the mercy of God is shown. They would never be happy in a perfect Heaven. Satan leads the whole multitude of fallen beings in a futile attack on the Holy City. As they do, fire comes down from God out of Heaven and devours them. Each one of them has their life preserved only long enough for them to pay for their sins. [20:9,12,13.] Satan is the last to die. In the Bible hell is another name for the grave. Even Satan doesn't burn forever. The Greek word for 'ever' is aeon. This word is better translated as 'an age.' I know this because death and hell [the grave] are cast into the lake of fire. There will be no more suffering or death in all of God's perfect Kingdom."

"If we never die what will we do with all the time we have in eternity Granddad?" **Remington** enquires.

"That's a study for another time. Do you feel better now Lulu?"

"Yes thanks Granddad. I'll be so glad when Jesus comes and there will eventually be no more death." Replies **Louise.**

"Me too. God bless children. Wash up now, it's time for tea."

GRANDDAD STORIES 8

DISCOURAGEMENT

"Hi children. Have you ever heard the story of Elijah? It is really exciting. First he told king Ahab that it wouldn't rain until he said so, and it didn't. That made king Ahab very mad. Elijah and God were on very good terms so that God spoke to him directly. After three years of drought God told Elijah that it was going to rain. First, Elijah had a meeting with king Ahab. He made it very clear to the king that the drought was brought about because Israel had abandoned God and was worshipping the false god Baal. [1 Kings 18:18.] They were going to have a showdown, Elijah and his God against Baal and his 450 prophets. The showdown was to take place on Mt. Carmel. All Israel gathered there. Here was the challange. Elijah asked, 'How long will you go limping between two different opinions? If the Lord is God, follow Him; but if Baal, then follow him.' In order to test who was truely God, Elijah said, let 2 alters be built and two bulls be killed, cut in pieces and put on the alters, but do not light a fire under it. We will both call on the name of the God we worship. The God Who answers by fire from Heaven, He is God." [1 Kings 18:23,24.]

"That's quite a test Granddad. With 450 prophets of Baal, couldn't one of them sneak some fire under their sacrifice?" **Louise** wanted to know.

"Elijah told them to go first. He was carefully watching all that they did. They danced around the alter all morning and lept and shouted saying, 'O Baal, hear us,' but there was no answer. At noon Elijah mocked them by saying, 'Cry louder. He might be thinking, or gone to the toilet, or on a journey, or asleep.' They yelled louder and cut themselves so that blood gushed out all over them. Finally they were totally exhausted. It was Elijahs turn." [1 Kings 18:26-29.]

"What did Elijah do Granddad?" **Remington** asked.

"He rebuilt the alter of the Lord that was broken down using 12 stones, one stone for each of the tribes of Israel. Then he dug a trench around the alter, put wood on the alter and laid his sacrifice on the wood. [1 Kings 18:30-32.] He had 12 barrels of water poured over the wood and the sacrifice, and the water filled the trench below the alter. That makes it very hard to start a fire, right? Remember, there had been a drought for three years and water was very scarce. [1 Kings 18:33-35.] Then he prayed a simple prayer; 'Hear me O Lord, that these people may know that you are the Lord God in

Israel.' Then fire came down from God out of Heaven and consumed the offering, the wood, the stones and the water that was in the trench. [1 Kings 18:36-38.] The people were so amazed that they bowed down and worshipped God right there and then. Then Elijah arrested all the prophets of Baal and killed every single one of them." [1 Kings 18:39,40.]

"That's so exciting Granddad. Is that the end of the story?" **Remington** wanted to know.

"Not quite. When king Ahab told queen Jezabel that Elijah had killed all her prophets, she had a fit. She was so mad that she sent a messenger to Elijah to say that she was after him, and that he'd be dead before tomorrow. [1 Kings 19:1,2.] Elijah had just won a mighty victory for God over 450 prophets of Baal. Do you think he'd let the threats of a woman bother him? Too right he did. He ran and ran all day, and when he finally stopped running he wanted to die. Well, you can read the rest of the story in 1 Kings 19, how the Lord fed him and got him out of his depression. Let me ask you this, what changed? What made Elijah turn from being a mighty champion for God to a man so scared of the threats of a woman that he ran for his life? Any ideas?"

Louise showed wisdom beyond her years. "When Elijah was fighting for God, all of his attention was on God and what he was doing. When he ran he was thinking only about himself. He lost his faith in God. All he could see was the threat to kill him."

"That's spot on Lulu. Someone else who went through that was the apostle Peter. He saw Jesus walking on water and asked Jesus if he could too. Jesus told him to come. While his eyes were on Jesus he was fine. As soon as he took his eyes off Jesus he sank. He allowed fear and doubt to weaken his trust in Jesus. [Matt. 14:28-31.] **In life, as long as our eyes are on Jesus we will be ok.** If we start thinking about ourselves we will become vain or proud or discouraged and depressed."

"John the Baptist was the same as Peter. He was in prison. Alone in that cell Satan was able to suggest all sorts of wrong things to him. His faith grew dim and he started to doubt Jesus. Like with Peter and Elijah, Jesus was able to strengthen John's faith."

Remington wanted to know, "did Jesus ever get discouraged?"

"Good question mate. Jesus had to go through a mock trial, His face was slapped, He was spat upon. He was mocked and whipped twice in the most horrible way; had a crown of thorns pressed deep into His skull and finally crucified, completely naked. Do you think that that would be enough to get Him discouraged? Matt. 27:46 tells us that He cried out, 'My God, My God, why have you forsaken Me?' For all of His life Jesus had a wonderful relationship with God. Many times they would chat all night. On the cross He couldn't sense the presence of the Father with Him any more. Jesus was paying for all of the sins of all mankind for all time on the cross. He was dying the second death in our place so thet we wouldn't have to. At the cross Jesus was being mocked and laughed to scorn by the priests and people and soldiers. [Psalm 22:7.] All His friends had deserted Him, except John and some women."

"But how did Jesus get over feeling down with all that going on," **Louise** asked.

"He stopped Himself from thinking about how bad things were for Him and started thinking about the good things He had done to help other people. Then He remembered His Father and started to praise Him. He remembered that, because of what He had done, people all over the world would turn to God and praise and worship Him." [Psalm 22:27.]

"Sometimes kids at school can be mean to you and say nasty things. Sometimes they say bad things on the internet like, you're useless; you're no good; nobody likes you. Sometimes people who are supposed to love you are always putting you down and you start to think that you *are* worthless. Just remember, **Jesus made you and Jesus doesn't make junk.**

He died for you so to Him you are of great worth. When you feel hurt or discouraged, try to think of all the good things God has given you in life, and praise Him for it. Try to do something good to help other people. Above all, pray. Before you know it you will no longer be sad. Just remember, Jesus loves you, and so do I. Bye children. God bless.

GRANDDAD STORIES 9

PROPHECY

"Hi Granddad." The children have come to visit for the weekend.

Remington asked, "Granddad, you said you could show us how we could trust the Bible because of prophecy. How can you do that?"

"Bible predictions, called prophecies were given so that, when they come true we have evidence that we can trust the Bible. We will have a look at a long prophecy that is still being fulfilled today, and along the way we'll have a bit of fun."

"Our key text will be Rev. 17:10, 11. There are 7 kings, 5 fallen, one still here and one yet to come. Then there's an 8th which is of the 7. Sounds like a real riddle, doesn't it?" Two things will help us out: one is to know that you can't read the Bible like a novel and think you know it all. Just as an artist will start with a sketch, add shape, add colour until the painting is finished, so does the Bible use this layering technique. It gives an overview in one chapter, fleshes it out with more detail in another and finishes the story in another book. Second, history will bear out what the Bible says, so that you can be sure that it is true."

"This sounds like fun Granddad." Enthused **Louise**.

"Here is an important point. **The Bible is a history of God's people.** There were other empires but the Bible is mainly concerned about God's people, their rebellion and what God did to bring them back again."

"We'll start in the second chapter of Daniel. In verse one the king, Nebuchadnezzar had a dream that greatly troubled him, but he couldn't remember the dream or what it meant. Finally Daniel came to the king with an answer to what his dream was and it's meaning. The king saw a huge statue, head of pure gold, chest and arms of silver, trunk of brass, legs of iron and feet of iron and clay. A large stone cut from the mountain of God without hands and smashed the statue on the feet and ground it to powder, which was blown away by a mighty wind. The stone grew to be a great mountain which covered all the Earth."

"In 2:29 Daniel tells the king that the dream concerned the future. In verse 38 Daniel reveals to the king, "you are this head of gold." In prophecy kings equals kingdoms. This dream is about world empires that would come and go. Babylon was the head of gold, the first of our 7 kingdoms.

There were to be 3 other world empires to arise and fall. After the forth there would be no more empires, but still 3 kings to come after the fourth empire. We will come back to this chapter. Let's go to chapter 7 in Daniel."

"Another dream, different images but the same meaning. Dan. 7:17. This time there are 4 beasts that come out of the sea. The first was a lion with eagles wings. This is Babylon. The second was a bear with 3 ribs in its mouth, the third was a leopard with 4 wings and the fourth beast that was so ferocious that there was nothing in nature to compare to it. From the head of this 4th beast grew 10 horns and a little horn that grew from the midst of them which uprooted 3 horns in its growth. Dan. 7:4-8. It spoke great things against the Most High God and persecuted His people. Again we'll come back to this chapter. Let's go to chapter 8 to see if we can identify more kings/kingdoms."

"Many years later Daniel had another dream. Babylon had been conquered and was gone. Now he dreams of a ram with 2 horns and a male goat that arises and pummels the ram. The goat had a prominent horn that was broken off and four smaller horns grew in its place. {vv 3-8.} In verse 20 we are told that the ram with 2 horns is the kings of Media and Persia. This kingdom of Medo/Persia is the chest and arms of silver in chapter 2 and the bear of chapter 7. In verse 21 we discover that our 3rd kingdom is Greece. Greece is the trunk of brass in the statue of Daniel 2 and the leopard of chapter 7. Are you keeping count children?"

"Yes Granddad. The three kings so far are Babylon, Medo/Persia and Greece. Is that right?" replies **Remington.**

"Very good. History tells that Medo/Persia conquered Babylon in 539 B.C. Greece conquered Medo/Persia in 331 B.C. Alexander the Great was their king. After he died at age 33, his 4 generals fought it out with each other. Finally one became victorious, Diadochi. So where did the fourth beast come from? Lucius Mummis was the Roman general who conquered Greece in 168 B.C., thus bringing forth the most brutal period in history to that point, the Roman empire. In Daniel 2 it is represented by the legs of iron. In chapter 7 it is the ferocious beast."

Now for titles. When Medo/Persia conquered Babylon it inherited the title, 'Babylon the great.' This title was passed on to Greece, then to Rome. Rome is also known in prophecy as 'the beast' as well as 'Babylon the Great.'

"So these are our 4 world empires that captured Gods people: Babylon; Medo/Persia; Greece and Rome."

"What happens next Granddad?" **Louise** was getting excited.

"Eventually Rome was conquered by savage tribes and western Rome was divided up into smaller countries which we call Europe today. Chapter 2 rightly refers to Europe as being partly strong and partly weak as iron doesn't mix with clay. We are told something very interesting in

chapter 2:43, that **Europe shall never be reunited.** Over the centuries many people have tried to conquer Europe to reunite it; people such as Charlemagne in 771 A.D. Charles V in 1530, King Louis XIV in the early 1700's, Napoleon in the early 1800's, Kaiser Wilhelm from 1914-1918 and Adolf Hitler from 1939-1945. These all failed. **God said no.** Queen Victoria became known as the grandmother of Europe because she tried to reunite Europe by marrying off her children to all the royal houses of Europe. She failed. **God said no.** Governments have tried economic means such as the Euro currency to reunite Europe. That failed. **God said no.** As long as Europe remains divided it is living proof that **God's Book is true,** it never changes. It is always reliable in every generation. After telling us that Daniel says that God will set up a Kingdom that will last forever. Now let's see what chapter 7 says."

"Wow Granddad, this is exciting. What else can happen?" enthused **Louise.**

"Are you ready for the 5th king? Here he comes. Let's have a look in Daniel 7:24 and onwards. In verse 24 we are told that the 10 horns are 10 kings or kingdoms. As with the 10 toes of Daniel 2 these also represent the 10 kingdoms of western Europe after the fall of Rome. From among these 10 horns a little horn grows, supplanting 3 horns in its growth. These 3 horns were the countries of the Vandals, the Ostrogoths and the Herili. These nations disappeared from history.

This little horn has a mouth that speaks great words against God. Who does that remind you of children?"

"Satan." answers **Remington.**

"The devil always works through people and organizations. This little horn power was, and is, his instrument to defy God. The little horn is no longer a political power only but a **religio/political** power. It now bears the titles of 'the Beast' and 'Babylon the Great', but also has added to this title, 'MYSTERY' Babylon the great.' He thinks he can change God's times and laws and persecutes to death the people of God. He is allowed to have control for a time, times and half a time. A time is a year, so that is 3 1/2 years. In Bible prophecy a day equals a year. 3 1/2 literal years equals 1,260 days. A day for a year is 1,260 years. [Numbers 14:34.] This is how long the little horn power had control, starting in 538 A.D. and ending in 1798. It happened this way. In 321 A.D. Constantine accepted Christianity as the religion of state. To make the pagans happy he made Sunday a day of rest instead of Sabbath. He also kept idol worship by changing the names of pagan gods like Jupiter, Juno and Minerva to Christian names like Peter, John and Mary. This pleased the Roman church. Constantine moved his capital from Rome to Constantinople and left the bishop of the church of Rome in charge. This church readily adopted the changes he made. By so doing it became an abomination to God. Theodosius 1 was the first Pope in the Byzantium era. In 538 emperor

Justinian enacted laws to persecute those who observed the 7th day Sabbath instead of Sunday. Thus began the 1,260 years of persecution for Gods faithful people. From this point on the faithful Christian church has become Gods chosen people instead of the Jewish nation and the devil works through corrupt churches to destroy the church"

"So the Roman church is the 5th king?" enquired **Louise.**

"Yes dear, that is my understanding. Let's see if all the pieces fit to identify the Roman church as the 5th king? When the emperor left Rome to the church of Rome, he handed to her the titles that belonged to pagan Rome. The church now became the 'Beast' and 'Babylon the Great, with the word 'Mystery' added to it. Did the Roman church speak great words against God? Yes. She claimed the right to forgive sin, something only Christ as our Redeemer can do. She charges money for people to escape punishment and to enter Heaven. How blasphemous. She violates the laws of God by omitting the 2nd commandment to not worship idols and splits the tenth commandment to make up the number. She claims that without the authority of Scripture she changed the day of worship from Sabbath to Sunday. She boasts that all who keep Sunday are showing allegiance to Rome. This is the mark of her authority, the mark of the Beast. Between 538 and 1798 she persecuted and killed between 50,000,000 - 150,000,000 people for their faith."

Remington was thoughtful. "Wow Granddad, Roman Catholics must be pretty rotten people?"

"Not at all. Many Catholics are among the most sincere and beautiful Christian people you could hope to meet. There is much we could learn from them in their piety and devotion to what they believe. I would love to be able to pray with the sincerity and fervour of a Catholic. It is the system that is wrong. Many dedicated Catholics have tried to improve the system from the inside from Huss to Luthor to the Wesleys, but many lost their lives in the attempt."

"Let's leave Daniel now and go to Revelation. Let's look at chapter 13:2. Here John sees a composite beast of lion, bear, leopard and the dragon gave this beast its power. In chapter 12:3 this dragon also appears. In 12:9 it is identified as Satan. In Bible prophecy a woman represents a church. A pure woman equals a pure church as in Rev. 12, which describes the beginning of the Christian church. In 17:18 we are told that the impure woman represents the great city, Rome, that reigns over the kings of the earth."

"There was one more thing about the 5th king. This church received a deadly wound that was healed. The wound happened in 1798 when Napoleon's general, Berthier captured the pope and confiscated the property belonging to the church. The Roman church lost political power as well as property of their own. The deadly wound began to heal when Mussolini signed a pact with the Vatican in 1929, creating an independent state of the Vatican city under the rulership of the pope. The Roman church's influence has steadily grown since then."

"After the pope was captured we entered into a period where secularism in various forms became the dominant belief in many countries. Evolutionary theory spread through the world and was rapidly accepted by secular people who denied God. Now it has infiltrated various churches as well. At the same time Communism gained power in Russia, China, Cuba and several other countries. Communists are totally secular in their beliefs. In 1793, God's 2 witnesses of the Old and New Testaments were banned from France for 3 1/2 years. In their place France inserted an impure woman and called her the goddess of reason in their assemblies. After 3 1/2 years the Bible was reinstated in France, just as the prophecy of Rev. 11 said."

"So where are we up to now children. How is our king count going?"

"We're up to 6 Granddad. Babylon, Medo/Persia, Greece, Pagan Rome and the Papal Rome are the kings that are fallen. Secularism in its many forms now rule. What's next Granddad?" asked **Louise.**

"Before Papal Rome received its deadly wound it had children. Many of the Protestant churches came out of the Catholic church. They include Church of England, Lutheran, Presbyterian, Methodist, Congregational etc. Originally God used these churches to reveal long buried Bible truths. As time went on protestant churches stopped protesting and compromised their distinctive beliefs."

"Let's pick up the story in Rev. 17:5. We know now who 'Mystery Babylon the Great' is, right? In this verse she is presented as an impure woman who had impure children. Let's track down these children. Rev. 13:3 tells us that the Beast [Papal Rome] received a deadly wound. This wound was healed and all the world was amazed. When the Beast is fully restored it will again continue its war against God with blasphemy and persecution of the saints of God. [13:6,7.] The end game of this power is worldwide domination and reverence and worship of the Papal system. In America and western nations apostate protestant churches will align with the Catholic system to compel all people to fall into line with Catholic doctrine. [vv. 11-15.]"

"So our 7th king is apostate Protestantism?" **Remington** was sure he was on the right track.

"Well done Rem. The dragon, Satan empowered the 'Beast', the Papal church, who in turn empowered the false prophet, the apostate churches, also known as the 'image to the beast,' and they all turned against the faithful followers of God to persecute and destroy them."

"That's terrible Granddad!" **Remington** was really afraid now.

"Don't worry Rem, I have good news. In chapter 18 John gives a call for all to come out of false systems of worship who want to be saved. He also says that False systems of worship will come to their end very unpleasantly in a very short time. In chapter 19:1,2 we discover that **GOD WINS! YAY!** God will only let apostacy go so far before He steps in to solve the problem. His ways are always true and just."

"I guess then the 8th king which is of the 7 is the church of Rome?" guessed **Louise.**

"Well done Lulu. You are correct. In Rev. 13:16, the mark of the Beast referred to is all about worship. The corrupt systems compel all people to worship on the false sabbath, Sunday. God's true people worship on God's true Sabbath in memory of Creation as God commanded. It is the Seal of God."

"That's all for now children. I hope it all makes sense to you."

"That was great Granddad. We've learned so much today. Thanks Granddad. The Bible really is fun to learn." enthused **Louise** for both of them.

"See you next time children. God bless."

GRANDDAD STORIES 10

QUESTIONS

"Hi Granddad, this is Ben. He heard we were having a Bible study and he has a few questions he'd like answered. We told him that you know everything. Is it ok for him to join us today?" Ben was a friend of **Louise's** from school.

"Two things, I wouldn't say I know everything, but the Bible does, and does your mother know you're here Ben?"

Ben had a note from his mother. "In that case, welcome Ben. What is your first question?"

Ben asked, "The Bible tells us that if we get our face slapped on one side then we have to offer the other side to be slapped as well. [Matt. 5:39.] If someone hits me am I just supposed to take it?"

"Ah yes, persecution. When some people know that you love Jesus they will go out of their way to make life hard for you. If you snap and are mean back to them, they can say that your faith is no good because you're just as bad as they are.

When someone is mean to you because of your faith, God is using you to be His champion. People will judge God by what they see in you. Do you know the best way to get back at someone who is mean to you? Be nice to them. It will make them feel rotten for the way they've treated you, or at least they might not be quite so mean next time. How can you hate someone who is always being nice. Even if they don't change at all at least you have shown the love of Christ. Jesus had the same problem. In John 15:18 He tells us that the world hated Him before it hated us. Jesus says in Matt. 5:10-12 that we are blessed when we are treated badly for His sake. We are to rejoice and be really glad for we have a great reward in Heaven. When we are treated like that because of our faith we have joined a very noble band, including the prophets, the apostles and Jesus. A good group to belong to. So remember, if someone is mean to you, be nice."

"That's not easy to do Granddad." observed **Remington.**

"No, but often it works, and sometimes you make a new friend."

Ben wanted to know, "but why do bad things happen to good people?"

"Sometimes it's their own fault or sometimes someone else causes the problem. Sometimes we are used by God to defend Him without even knowing it. God uses us and the bad that happens to us to do good for others."

"Really? Like what?" **Louise** couldn't believe it.

"I will show you from Scripture. In the old Testament there was a man named Job who was a champion for God. He was rich with 7 sons and 3 daughters and lots of servants and camels and sheep and donkeys and cattle. Everybody loved each other and they all loved God and hated evil. [Job 1:8.] One day Satan said to God, 'Job only loves you because You bless him and protect him. Take away his possessions and he will curse You to Your face.' [Job 1:11.] God told Satan that all Job had was in his hands. Just leave Job himself alone. Satan was very happy. He attacked Job with everything he had. All his livestock were stolen in raids, buildings were destroyed and, worst of all, every one of Job's 10 children were killed." [Job 1:14-19.]

"Wow! What did Job do?" asked **Ben.**

"He tore his clothes in grief, shaved his head in mourning and fell on the ground and worshipped God. He said, 'the Lord gave, the Lord has taken away. Blessed be the name of the Lord.' Remember kids, it wasn't God who did all that to Job, it was Satan. Job didn't know that." [Job 1:20,21.]

"Remington wanted to know, "then what happened?"

"Satan and God had another chat. God asked Satan, 'so how's Job going? Has he cursed Me yet?' Satan had to say no, but added, 'touch his bone and his flesh and then he will curse you to your face.' God said, 'ok, just don't kill him.' [Job 2:6.] So Satan struck Job all over his body, head to foot with loathsome boils. Even his wife had had enough. She said to him, 'do you still trust God? Curse Him and die.' He told her that she speaks as a foolish woman. They were happy to be with God in the good times, why should they abandon Him in bad times."

"Three of Job's friends came along and tried to convince Job that what he was going through was all his fault. He must have sin in his life to be punished like that. I love what Job told them. He said, 'though He slaye me, yet will I trust Him... He also shall be my salvation.' [Job 13:15,16.] I'll say just one more thing about Job. After all the trials and losses he went through he was still faithful to God, and God was able to bless him with twice as much as he had before in livestock and possessions. Job and his wife had another 7 sons and 3 daughters. Satan was defeated. Job was a worthy champion for God. Job can look forward to seeing his first family again when Jesus comes." [Job 42:12,13.]

"That's some story Granddad. I'm glad that it didn't happen to me." declared **Louise**.

"Would you like to hear about another champion for God who Jesus used to teach the disciples a good lesson? She was a Greek woman. She came to see Jesus and asked Him to cast a demon out of her daughter. [Mark 7:26.] He ignored her. Have you ever been to someone for help, only to be ignored? [Matt. 15:23.] Did you stay around that person for long? She did. She kept pleading. Jesus finally told her, 'I didn't come here to help you, only the lost sheep in Israel.' [Matt. 15:24.] Have you ever been to someone for help, only to be told that they wouldn't help you? Did you stay around that person for long? Did you worship that person? She did, and she kept pleading with Him for help. Jesus then told her, ' it's not right to take the children's bread and give it to dogs.' Have you ever been to someone for help, only to be told you are a dog? Did you stay around that person for long? She did. She answered Him, 'that's true, but even the dogs eat of the crumbs that fall from the master's table.' [Matt.15:26, 27.] She was saying, 'if I am a dog I am entitled to some dog food.' Jesus said, 'oh woman, great is your faith' and her daughter was healed. She didn't accept on face value what Jesus was telling her, but she DID trust Him. Why did Jesus put that foreign woman through all that? It was to show the disciples that they are wrong to despise foreigners and to judge them as inferior and unworthy of salvation or help. She was Jesus's champion. Bad things happened for good reasons and she was well rewarded in the end. We need to trust God more in all cases, good or bad."

"All right, what about where Jesus says that if you want more money then you should give away what you have? That doesn't make sense." **Ben** was sure he had Granddad this time.

"You must remember, God owns everything, including you and all that you have. He made you and bought you back again with the blood of Jesus. You only get to use your stuff for a while. So when God says to give a tenth of what you earn to Him, he also promises to give you such a blessing if you do, that you won't have room enough to receive it." [Malachi 3:8-10.]

"A rich, young ruler came to Jesus asking what he needed to do to be saved. He thought he was pretty good. Jesus told him that he lacked one thing. He told him to sell all that he had and give the money to the poor, then he will have treasure in Heaven. Jesus wanted this guy to follow Him. [Mark 10:21.] The rich, young ruler couldn't do it. He loved his money too much. Silly, it is so easy to loose it here. I almost lost $10,000 to scammers. I got it back, but it shows that money is not safe here. Better to use it to help people get to know Jesus and find salvation."

"Jesus said if you have 2 coats and you meet someone who doesn't have a coat, you are to give him one of yours. [Luke 3:11.] I guess if you practice sharing your stuff with others like that, it would be hard to become selfish, wouldn't it Granddad?" **Louise** observed.

"You've got it Lulu. Whatever the Bible asks you to do is for your benefit and to help others. It's always for good, and you will never be the poorer for doing it. For instance, Jesus said that anyone who wants to be the greatest among you should become the greatest servant. [Matt. 23:11.] It is hard to big note yourself when you're doing the serving, and others benefit from your work. God's ways may seem strange to our way of thinking at times but how wise they are when properly understood. When we give ourselves to Jesus we also give Him all our money and all our possessions, to use however He wants to use them. How great it is to know that God will not only look after us but also use us to look after others."

"I think that will do for now. If you have other questions feel free to ask them next time. God bless children."

"Thank you Granddad. Bye for now." **Remington** spoke for all the children.

GRANDDAD STORIES 11

THE SANCTUARY

"Granddad, you have already told us about a long time prophecy. Is that the longest time prophecy there is in the Bible?" **Louise** wanted to know.

"In Daniel 8:14 we are told, 'until two thousand, three hundred days, then shall the Sanctuary be cleansed.' That is almost twice as long as the 1,260 year prophecy that we have already looked at. Buckle up kids and pay close attention, because this subject gets a little involved. I will try to explain it to you as simply as I can so that you can understand it. To properly understand this message we need to remember that in Bible time prophecies, one day equals one year. So 2,300 days is covering 2,300 years in real time. That is a long time, but the Bible breaks it up into several sections."

"'Seventy weeks are determined upon thy people....' They had seventy weeks; 490 years to do what God wanted them to do, otherwise they would cease to be God's chosen people as a race. Their sins were such that, without immediate and drastic reform, God would no longer be able to use Israel to tell the world of the wonderful love He had for them. The 70 weeks are broken up into two sections - 69 weeks and one week. God wanted them to stop sinning and to atone for their sins. He wanted them to again be a Holy and righteous people, and to repair the Temple of the Lord, and to anoint the Most Holy, Jesus, as the Messiah." [Daniel 9:24.]

"So when do the 2,300 day/years start"? **Remington** asked.

"Daniel 9:25 gives the answer. It says, 'From the going forth of the command to restore and to build Jerusalem until Messiah the Prince [Jesus] shall be in total sixty nine weeks. Sixty nine weeks is 483 days/years. To answer your question Rem, there were three decrees given by the Persians to rebuild Jerusalem, but the one that was acted upon was given by king **Artaxerxes** in 457 B.C. That is our starting point. Go forward 483 years and that brings us right up to the baptism of Jesus by John in 31 A.D. That is when Jesus became 'Messiah, the Prince.'

"But that's only 69 weeks. What about the 70th week of the prophecy." asked a puzzled **Louise.**

"This week was also split in half. From A.D. 31, after His baptism, Jesus had just 3 1/2 years to tell the people what God was really like and to show them the true way to Heaven. At the end of that time He would stop the killing of animals as sacrifices to God because He, Himself would become God's Sacrifice for sin forever. 3 1/2 years later, after Jesus was crucified, the Christian church had grown a lot, but was still a Jewish Christians church. The last straw for Israel to be God's chosen people came in 38 A.D. when Stephen became the first Christian martyr, stoned to death by the Jews. [Acts 7:58, 59.] That ended the 70 weeks or 490 years. From then on, the Gospel went to the Gentiles. [Acts 13:46.] For the next 1,810 years part of the prophecy, we have the Christian era when Jesus was our High Priest in Heaven; the Holy Spirit was looking after God's people in the midst of savage persecution, and the established churches became more and more corrupt under Satan's leadership. This prophecy finished in the spring of 1844, exactly 2,300 years after the decree was given to restore Jerusalem. God's timing is perfect."

Louise asked, "In 457 B.C., at the start of the prophecy; something happened. The Jews were sent back to Israel to rebuild the walls and the city and the temple. In 31 A.D. something happened; Jesus was baptized. 3 1/2 years later something happened; Jesus was crucified. In 38 A.D. something happened; Stephen was stoned. What happened in 1844?"

"Toward the end of the 2,300 years there was a period of great Christian revivals. People all over the world started preaching the same message at about the same time, based solely on Scripture. There was Joseph Wolf in Asia, Catholic priests in Latin America, Anglican ministers in England, and a farmer named William Miller in America. Miller read Daniel 8:14 and figured that the Earth was the Sanctuary to be cleansed. He concluded that Christ was to return in 1844. The time came and went. Everyone were bitterly disappointed. Many abandoned their faith. Some went back to the Bible to find out what went wrong. They discovered that, in the Bible, the Earth is described as God's foot stool, not His Sanctuary." [Isa. 66:1.] God knew this little flock would be discouraged, so He sent them a message in Rev. 10:9-11. It was sent by a mighty angel. This means that a message of great importance was being given. The angel had a little book in his hand that had been sealed, [Dan. 12:4.] but was now opened. The book of Daniel is for our time. In vision John was told to eat the book. In his mouth it would be as sweet as honey, but in his belly it would be bitter. The experience of believers pre 1844 was so beautiful, expecting and planning for Jesus to come. The Bible calls this message, 'the Loud Cry.' [Matt. 25:5, 6.] When that didn't happen their experience was bitter with disappointment and ridicule. They were encouraged by the instruction to them in Rev. 10:11. They were told that they must prophecy again to many nations, peoples, tongues and kings. They had their marching orders."

"Is that when Ellen White was alive. I have heard many people refer to her as the Spirit of Prophecy. Is that right Granddad?" **Louise** enquired.

"Ellen White did live then. She was a wonderful and dedicated woman. God gave her many gifts and abilities, so that she was able to establish churches and confirm the faith of many. To Ellen was given the gift of prophecy. Was she, and are her writings, the Spirit of Prophecy spoken of in Rev. 19:10? **No.** That title belongs only to the Holy Spirit. [2 Peter 1:20, 21.] Her roll was more like that of an apostle, establishing, guiding, reproving and encouraging churches. She was never the leader of a denomination. She was one of many people God used to establish and direct a people with a vital message for these last days; that Jesus is coming very soon. That means that God's people of the last days will be filled with the Holy Spirit and will be obedient to God by obeying His commandments."

"But Granddad, didn't the text say that the Sanctuary would be cleansed after 2,300 days/years? By then there was no Sanctuary left to cleanse. It had been destroyed by Titus in 70 A.D." Now **Remington** was also puzzled.

"That is true. To understand this we need to go back to the Jewish Sanctuary and see how that worked. Every day when someone sinned, they would bring a sacrifice to the temple, place their hands on the victim's head and confess their sins. Then they would take a knife and slit it's throat."

"Oh, how horrible." screamed **Louise.**

"Yes it was, but God designed this process to teach the people just how deadly sin really was, and still is. As the blood was pumping out of the animal the priest would collect some of the blood and sprinkle it before the veil of the Sanctuary. [Leviticus 4:4-6.] What was really happening was that the sins of the person were transferred from the sinner to the sacrifice via the blood, then from the sacrifice to the temple via the blood. This went on every day of the year. The Day of Atonement was judgement day for the people. All sins had to be confessed and forsaken by then. Finally the High Priest chose two goats. One was called the Lord's goat. This goat was sacrificed as a final atonement for the people of Israel. That goat represented Christ, and what He would do to save us from our sins. The second goat was called the scape goat. Symbolically, all of the sins of Israel that had been collected in the temple throughout the year were now placed on the head of the scape goat. This goat represented Satan. He will finally bear the sins of all the people and angels that he influenced to sin against God. That goat was to be lead into the wilderness by a strong man and released. [Lev.16:7-10.] Thus the temple was cleansed from all sin and the people could begin a new year sin free,"

"That was fine for them, but what temple is being cleansed now?" a very confused **Remington** asked.

"Don't you see? Even though there is a Sanctuary in Heaven after which the Earthly Tabernacle was patterned, [Hebrews

8:2.] this is not about buildings. It is about what Jesus is doing to get rid of the sin problem once and for all. When Jesus went to Heaven, He received all of the prayers and requests for forgiveness of the people on Earth. In 1844 Jesus entered a second phase of the plan of redemption. The symbolic record books were opened, [Rev. 20:12.] and everyone was judged from what was written in their life record. Some were found to be without a wedding garment - the righteousness of Christ. They will not see Heaven. Some seemed to be on fire for Christ here, but in their hearts they were using church as a fire insurance policy. They knew ABOUT Christ but they didn't know Him as a true Friend. To such Jesus has to say, 'depart from me ye accursed, I never knew you.' They won't see Heaven either. Then, there are some who have never heard the story of Jesus and His love for them, but they have lived according to all the light that God had given them. They will be saved, in that, if they had had the chance to know Jesus, they would have. [Romans 2:14, 15.] Finally, everyone will be judged and their eternal fates decided. The saved will rise to everlasting life when Jesus comes. [Rev. 20:4, 6.] After a thousand years the dammed will be brought back to life to receive their judgement. Then fire will come down from God out of Heaven and consume all sinners, including fallen angels. [Rev. 20:15.] Each being will live only until they have paid for their sins, then they will die permanently. The last one to die will be Satan. Death and hell [the grave] were also cast into the lake of fire. Death is forever finished after Satan dies. He is by far the greatest sinner. At last all sin will be cleansed from the universe and then there will be no more tears nor crying, no more pain. [Rev.21:4.] No one will even want to sin again and peace and love will reign forevermore."

GRANDDAD STORIES 12

REVELATION

Remington wanted to know, "why is the book of Revelation so hard to understand Granddad?"

"Good question. God saw that if He had John speak plainly, the enemies of God would be so upset to see their plans exposed that they would destroy the book. For this reason Revelation is written in code. The keys to understanding it are contained elsewhere in the Bible. Here is a vital point to remember. From beginning to end the Bible has only one story...... ***It is all about Jesus***......., what He's done for us and what He is still doing. All the blood and gore in the Bible shows how desperate He was to protect His people from corruption. Once you study the Bible and see Jesus, you can't help but fall in love with Him and want to serve Him with all your being."

"So how do we understand Revelation Granddad?" **Louise** asked.

"It is like a summary of all that has gone on in the rest of the Bible and what is yet to happen. The great news is that Jesus has the keys to death and the grave. He overcame death and He has the power to save all who trust in Him. Nothing can take from His hands those who trust in Him." [Rev. 14:13.]

"I love these Bible studies Granddad. They help me learn so much." enthused **Remington.**

"Many of the different symbols in Revelation tell the same story with different details. The 7 churches in Rev. 2, 3 were 7 literal churches. The messages were for them primarily. The second way to understand these messages is that they apply to 7 different time periods of the church. At first, the church was pure and without heresy. Then falsehood began to creep in. It got worse until the church was killing innocent, God-fearing people who wouldn't go along with the man-made falsehoods that the church was teaching. The 6th church was again pure and spotless. It was a time of great missionary activity, and the time of the great disappointment when Jesus was expected to come but didn't. That caused a period of intense Bible study to understand what went wrong. Now we are in the Laodicean period. [Rev. 3:14-21.] We are the church who thinks we have it all together, that we know everything from the Bible. [Rev. 3:17.] We do know a lot, but we are not doing much with that knowledge. That is why Jesus calls us lukewarm. [Rev. 3:16.] Some are sharing their faith, but most are just warming pews. Now let's see what remedy Jesus has for our condition. We will look at Rev. 3:18-20, the counsel to the Laodicea and the 3 angels messages of Rev.14:6-12."

Let's look at Rev. 3:18. The Laodiceans think that they are pretty good, but Jesus saw them as they really are. They are counselled to buy from God gold tried in the fire that they may be rich. Isaiah tells us to come to the waters to buy and drink, those without money. There is no cost. [Isa. 55:1, 2.] Jesus says that He is the Living Water. [John 4:14.] In Hebrews 11:6 we are told that without faith it is impossible to please God, for those who come to God must believe that He exists, and will reward those who diligently seek Him. So the gold that we need to 'buy' Christ, the living water, without money or price is **FAITH!"**

"White raiment is our next need. Isaiah says that all OUR righteousness are as filthy rags. [Isa. 64:6.] In Zechariah 3:2-4, God and Satan were having a debate over Joshua, the high priest. Standing before God in filthy rags Joshua was unworthy to be there. God, Himself provided Joshua with the clothes He needed. The parable of the wedding feast is another good example. There was a guest who refused to wear the provided wedding garment. He was bound and cast into outer darkness. So what clothing is suitable for Heaven? Our righteousness is no good, so the only righteousness that will enter Heaven is the righteousness of Christ. Jesus wants to change our characters so that we are no longer depending on ourselves and what we do to be saved, but rather we are depending on Him alone. Only He can provide us with His character if we let Him. We must 'put on' Christ through faith." [Galatians 3:27.]

"So what is the eyesalve Granddad?" **Louise** wanted to know.

"Eyesalve is designed to cure blindness. Laodicea is spiritually blind. The only cure for spiritual blindness is the Comforter, the Holy Spirit. He it is Who reproves the world of sin and righteousness and judgement. He it is Who will guide us into all truth. He will speak for, and glorify Christ."

"So we need gold - faith in Christ; white raiment - the righteous of Christ and eyesalve - the Holy Spirit, in order to be saved. Is that right Granddad?" **Remington** wanted to know.

"Spot on Rem. Now let's see how Rev. 14:6-12 says the same thing. Three angels which means three messages that God wants to give to the Earth."

"Angel 1 - Fear God and give glory to Him and worship Him. [Rev. 14:7.] In other words, have faith in God and worship Him."

"Angel 2 - Babylon is fallen. [Rev. 14:8.] We know from previous studies that Babylon is corrupt and false systems of worship. Those who follow her doctrines can never wear the white robe of God which is the righteousness of Christ."

"Angel 3 - For those who cling to the Satanic beliefs of the Beast and his image, that is, false worship, there is nothing but judgement and destruction. [Rev.14:9-12.] Those who obey God have had their eyes opened to the truth and are guided by the Holy Spirit. The Spirit leads them into all truth. [John 16:13.] In the last days the people of God will be filled with the Holy Spirit and will obey God in all things. [Rev. 14:12; 12:17.] God still has faithful people worshipping in fallen churches, not knowing of their falsehoods. Rightly does the angel from Heaven say, 'Come out of her, my people, that you will not be partakers of her sins.' [Rev. 18:4.] God is pleading with us to turn to Him, to allow the Holy Spirit to change our filthy characters into pure and holy characters by the righteousness of Christ, and to accept and love Him fully and to obey Him. He only asks us to do what is good for us and to help other people to find Jesus and be saved."

"Boy Granddad, that was pretty intense, but now I understand much clearer what those passages in Revelation are really saying. I can see also why John had to write in code." observes **Louise.**

"Yes Lulu, and it's so vital that we understand it as well. God bless children."

GRANDDAD STORIES 13

2ND COMING

"Granddad, you have told us how the Bible says that Jesus is coming back again soon, but what if He doesn't come? Some people are saying that it's just a story and that this life is all we have." **Louise** seemed troubled.

"Don't worry, He'll come. You can trust the Bible. It is always right."

"I know, but what if they're right? What if He doesn't come?" **Louise** insisted.

"O.k., Let's say your friends are right. Where does that leave us? The beliefs I have from the Bible teach me to love, respect and care for other people. I am to do what I can to help them when they need my help. My Beliefs from the Bible tell me to not lie nor be unfaithful to my wife nor to get angry with anyone without a good reason, and to respect my parents. My beliefs also tell me that it is not good to smoke or to drink or to use drugs not prescribed by a doctor. Also I am to look after my health through good diet and exercise and plenty of rest at night. I try to not stress and to keep everything in balance in my life, not getting too focused on one part and ignoring another part. For instance, I'm not so busy earning money that I don't pay much attention to my family. There are more important things in life than money. These are just a few benefits of being a Christian. Also, my faith gives me hope for something much better at the end of this life. I expect that, when I die, it will seem like just an instant later that I will open my eyes and see Jesus come. I will die happy. If Jesus doesn't come, I won't know it. I will have lived a good, productive life. That is if non-believers are right. Not a bad way to live, huh?"

"But what if the Bible is right and Jesus is coming to Judge every man and woman according to the works that they've done in this life? Where does that leave the non-believers? Without Jesus they have no hope. It is worth living the Christian life. It keeps me from so many of the problems that others bring on themselves through the choices they make, and I don't have to fear the judgement. I have already been found not guilty through Jesus."

"Jesus **is** going to come soon Granddad, I know He is." **Remington** was sure he was right.

Louise was curious, "Ok. So when is He going to come Granddad?"

"The Bible doesn't tell us exactly when Jesus is going to return. If it did some people would wait until the very last minute to get their lives in order. We are told to seek God's Kingdom and His righteousness today and to not worry about tomorrow. If we do that, God will look after our other needs like food and clothing." [Matt. 6:33,34.]

"Does the Bible give any hints about when Jesus will come?" asked **Louise.**

"Sure, lots of them. First, I want you to clearly understand something very important. Either we accept fully what Jesus and the Bible says or we believe the sceptics. If the sceptics are right then Jesus is a liar and a deceiver, not to be trusted. That is what is at stake here. Now let's see what Jesus actually said. In John 14:1-3 Jesus said, 'Don't let your hearts be troubled. You believe in God, believe in Me also. In My Father's house are many mansions. If it were not so, I would have told you. I go to prepare a place for you so that, where I am you can be there also.' When we turn to Matt. 24 the disciples asked Jesus the exact, same question - 'what will be the sign of your coming?' [Matt. 24:3.] In verse 7 Jesus says that there will be wars, famines, pestilences [like the Covit 19 virus.] and earthquakes."

"But we've always had those Granddad." **Louise** objected.

True, but they are becoming much more common now and they're happening all over the place. They're much worse than they've ever been before. Jesus said that these natural disasters are just the beginning of sorrows. [Matt. 24:8.] He warned that before the end those who love Jesus will be hated and betrayed and killed. He said that because there is so much sin around that many who once loved Jesus will give up and turn away from Him. I have seen that happen with people who were close to me. Then liars will come pretending to be from Jesus. They will say untrue things that many will believe and will be deceived. Jesus says to hang on to your faith until the end, then you will be saved."

"That sounds good Granddad, but what is the best sign that Jesus is about to come?" asked **Remington**.

"Matt. 24:14 has the answer. When the Gospel of the Kingdom has been preached in all the world so that everyone has had a chance to accept Jesus or not, then Jesus will come, and everyone will see Him coming, just as we see lightning flashes everywhere. [Matt. 24:27.]

"When Jesus was leaving the disciples, two angels said to them; 'men of Galilee, why are you staring up into heaven? This very same Jesus Who you saw go up from you into the sky will come in the same way as you saw Him go.' [Acts 24:11.] When Jesus comes it will be no secret thing. Everyone will see Him come physically from Heaven.

"When Jesus comes again, what will the people who don't love Jesus be doing Granddad?" **Remington** wanted to know.

"Revelation 1:7 says that when Jesus comes every eye will see Him, including those who were involved in His crucifixion. They must have been specially resurrected from the dead to witness the event. Then all people on Earth will wail and cry because of Him. They wil cry for the rocks and the mountains to fall on them and to hide them from the face of Jesus. [Rev. 6:15,16.] When Jesus comes it will not be a happy time for the sceptics and those who don't love Him. They will all die, killed by the brightness of the glory of Jesus and of all the angels."

Now **Louise** asks, "what will happen to the people who do love Jesus when He comes?"

"Paul tells us in 1 Thess. 4:13-18 that we are not to sorrow as those who have no hope sorrow. Jesus will descend from Heaven with a shout, with the voice of the archangel and the righteous dead will rise first. Then the righteous living will be caught up with the resurrected ones to meet Jesus in the air and will forever be with the Lord. I guess they travel by angel express. All saved will be given new, perfect bodies that will last forever." [1 Cor. 15:51-53.]

"Is that all the evidence you have Granddad?" **Louise** wanted to know.

"Not by any means. Do you remember our discussion on the prophecies of Daniel and Revelation? In Dan. 2:44,45 the statue was destroyed by that rock from the mountain of God, which is the 2nd coming of Jesus. In chapter 7:26,27 the little horn power is destroyed and the people of God inherit the Kingdom. In Rev. 22:20 Jesus Himself says that He is coming quickly. All these texts are just the end of a long prediction. All the other things predicted have come true. Why should we believe that this last part will not happen? Surely I come quickly Jesus said, and I believe Him."

"Does that answer your question Lulu?"

"Yes Granddad. It all makes sense now. I believe that Jesus is true and not a liar."

"That's wonderful. God bless children."

"Well dear readers, we've been on quite a journey from Genesis to Revelation. This is my final story for now. My prayer is that you may have read something that has increased your knowledge and understanding of the Scripture, and has brought you a little closer to Jesus as your Friend and Savior. **Jesus will come again.** When the Gospel of the Kingdom has been preached into all the world as a witness to all nations, it will happen. A good way for you to share your faith is to give these stories to someone else you care about. May God bless you as you serve Him."
Granddad Rob. 11/3/2021.

WAITING FOR HEAVEN.

When I think of Heaven so pure and undefiled,
free of every taint and trace of sin.
Lord I want to be there, I want to be your
child. I want eternal freedom to begin.

Jesus my redeemer, my comforter and king,
You are all my life, my dearest friend.
When you come in glory, then I know you'll
bring all of my sins and trials to an end.

Now I must be patient and wait for Your return.
While I wait there's much work to be done.
Reaching out to others, helping them to learn
to live their lives for Gods' Eternal Son.

Just to be with you lord, to see you every day,
to know I'm perfectly within your will..
All my pain and sorrow, all my heartache will be gone,
when in my mind you whisper peace, be still! be still!

© Rob Simmons.

IT'S NOT EASY LORD.

It's not easy Lord to love those who treat me so unkind.
Lord I want to turn away and just leave them all behind.
It's not easy Lord to care when rejection comes my way.
Help me Lord to understand and from them not turn away.

Though I don't deserve You Lord, still Your love for me is strong.
I want all the world to know that to you my life belongs.
Jesus teach me how to love? Show me how to be a friend?
Leading people Lord to You, to a life that never ends.

How can I be so unkind, when I think of all You've done
Lord You gave yourself for me, even though You're God the Son.
Lord I want to be like You. Give me victory o'er my sins.
Help me trust You more each day, 'till eternal life begins.

© Rob Simmons.

CAN YOU SEE HIM?

Have you ever wondered what to Jesus was the cost
To be fashioned as a human, so to seek and save the lost?
Did you know that to the Father He gave all that was His own?
His power, His perfection, His universe, His throne
To be born a helpless Baby that redemption may begin
With a form that was affected by four thousand years of sin?
Yet He willingly surrendered all into the Father's care
That with us He could be numbered, and
the Father's love could share.

Can you see Him as a youngster learning from His mother's knee
All the wonder of the Scriptures, all the truth's that told how He
Was to come and live among us as the Man who God had sent
That for us He'd give His life so that from sin we could repent?

Can you see Him as a young man healing
blind and lame and dumb,
Teaching them the way to Heaven, of that better land to come?
Can you see Him with the hypocrites, the Pharisees and Scribes,
Rebuking their hypocrisies, their flatteries and bribes?

Can you see His loving kindness to a sinner brought by some
Who would later crucify Him, though they couldn't even come
To Him with any accusation of a crime or anything
That would justify the killing of the Son of God, their King?

Can you see Him now with Pilate, or with Herod who would sneer,
Mocking, laughing, and accusing Him Who gave no sign of fear?
Can you see Him being beaten by rough men with whips of hide?
Can you see the led and iron gouging deep into His side?

Can you see Him bleeding, dying on that cruel cross of shame
For the very ones now scoffing and rejecting why He came?
Can you see Him being buried in a tomb that's not His own?
Can you see that precious head which for a pillow had a stone?

Can you see Him rise triumphant from
the grave that couldn't hold
The One who now had conquered death, the sweetest story told?
Can you see Him with the Father on His shining throne of gold
Planning soon for the redemption of His children, young and old?

Can you see Him come in glory? Can you see the saints arise
From their graves and imperfections to meet Jesus in the skies?
Now with Jesus e'er to reign in that sinless land, their home.
All because Jesus was willing to give up to God His throne.

© Rob Simmons. 1982.

BE MINE!

Dear little child alone and afraid,
Your life seems so hopeless to you.
All your troubles surround you like clouds in a storm.
There's heartache whatever you do. But...

Don't you know your Father really loves you?
And don't you know you are precious in My sight?
I poured out all of Heaven just to save you.
I'll make all of your problems turn out right.

Dear little child, though trembling you rise
In faith to begin life again.
You have heard that I love you, that I'm with you right now
And on Me you can always depend.

Dear little child, just look at you now.
Your faith has on eagles wings flown.
All the powers of hell cannot harm you My child,
For with Me you are never alone. For...

Don't you know just how much I really love you?
And don't you know your voice is music to My ears?
I poured out all of Heaven just to save you.
I want you to be with Me through the years.
Be Mine! Be Mine!

© Rob Simmons 1996.

LOVE AND RELATIONSHIPS.

GNANAMANI.

I've met a little lady who's lovely and kind,
A lady full of sunshine and life.
I love that little lady and I know she loves me,
So I'm gone and made her my wife.
Her smile is so inviting, so lovely and warm.
Her lips can drive me out of my mind,
And when I hold her in my arms there's nothing to fear,
I can leave my worries behind.

Me and my Gnanamani will worship our God,
We'll praise Him for the things he has done
He's given us each other and our lovely new home
Best of all He's given His Son.
Now me and Gnanamani are madly in love
We want to be together each day
And as the years go by we'll have each other to share,
To have and hold in every way.

Oh, she's my funny honey bunny lovey dovey Gnanamani.
She's my funny honey bunny lovey dovey Gnanamani.
Together we have made a home we can call our own Oh yeah!
It's for me and funny honey bunny lovey dovey Gnanamani

© Rob Simmons, 1997

SONG FOR IRENE.

For all my life I have searched for you.
No one has ever loved me as you do.
Now I have found who I've been searching for.
I will love you 'til forever more.

But, oh my darling, what have I to offer you?
What have I to match you lovin' heart?
I'll gladly give you all I have, and all I am
And nothing will ever keep us apart.

Irene darling, you are mine alone.
With my children we will make our home.
You bring me comfort and security.
Friend and lover, you're the world to me.

God has really given us the very best this time.
I am ever yours my love, and you are mine.
We'll grow old together, darlin' you and I.
Caring for each other as the years go by.

We will worship as we kneel and pray
Thanking God for every brand new day.
Then when in death we sleep the long, dark night,
I'll still love you in the morning's light.
I'll still love you in the morning's light.

© Rob Simmons.

THERE IS NO US WITHOUT YOU.

Alone I am lonely and wanting you only to
be here to share all my dreams.
It takes two to tango and even a mango tastes
better when shared, so it seems.
My partner for living, for loving and giving,
there's no "I" in team, so they say.
You bring me completeness, your love is the sweetness,
that makes me a happier man every day.

Together we invite, at morn or at midnight,
the Lord to be part or our lives.
He wants to live in us to shape us, prepare
us to meet Jesus when he arrives.
Soon Jesus is coming. There'll be no more
numbing, nor aching nor tears nor despair.
We'll look up together and know that forever we'll
be with our Savior and ever declare....

There is no us without you! To you I will ever be true.
You're with me to help me whatever I do,
'cause there is no us without you!

© Rob Simmons.

BEAUTIFUL!

We've been together quite a while now darling, you and I.
I guess the years that still remain will quickly pass on by.
We've talked, we've laughed, we've cried, we've
prayed through all that's come along.
For the time that still remains you'll be my joy and song.

Yes, you can be impatient and perhaps a little proud.
At times words have been spoken that should not be said aloud.
I know that I can be far worse and yet you love me still,
In spite of all my weaknesses, I hope you always will.

I draw a lot of comfort that you know me as you do.
When I am sad, determined, glad, you know me through and through.
The future may hold few surprises as we go through life.
I'll always thank the Lord above for making you my wife.

I have called you beautiful and beautiful you are.
Far greater than appearance, you are like the morning star
That brightens up the darkest nights and gladdens all my days.
You're everything I want my dear, today and for always.

You're my wife and you're my lover, my comfort and friend.
You have shown me that you are the one on whom I can depend.
You're my joy and inspiration, you brighten up my life,
And I thank the Lord for making you my wife.

© Rob Simmons. 18.12 2003.

YOU'RE DESIRABLE TO ME.

Time has come and gone and now I wonder
how I feel about the one I've wed.
Do you thrill me as you did that evening
as we lay upon our wedding bed.

Do I still enjoy your hugs and kisses, as I did so many years ago?
Do I boast to others of my missus? Well of
course I do that don't you know?

Do we still enjoy our time together as we
read and close our eyes to pray?
Knowing soon we'll share our love forever.
I don't want it any other way.

Time and age will never dim the love I have for you.
With the dawning of each day this love is born anew.

You are beautiful! You are wonderful! You're desirable to me.
You are home, my dear where there is no
fear. You're my peace and my safety.
You're my peace and my safety. You are everything to me.

© Rob Simmons. 01/09/04.

THE NEVERENDING ANNIVERSARY SONG.

[The number changes for each anniversary.]

When I gaze upon your face and see the
look of love that's in your eyes,
Again I realize the loveliness I see is no disguise.
The smile upon your face, the feel of your
embrace has chased away all fears.
Though it seems like just a day we've been together 23 years.

When I think of all the joy, the happiness
I've known since loving you.
To think it's but a taste of wondrous love
we'll share when all is new.
When Jesus comes again we'll spend eternity in perfect harmony.
Until then my darling one we'll be together, you and me.

23 years we have been together, 23 years you have shared my life.
Darling, having you with me and loving
you has been so great a pleasure
For the 23 years you have been my wife.

© Rob Simmons. April 2000.

I CHERISH YOU.

First I liked you, then I loved you, now I cherish you.
I know as we journey on together our love will always renew.
First you liked me, then you loved me, now you cherished me.
And just as time marches on forever, our love will ever be true.

I will spend my life with you my dear.
Our house will be our home just as long
as you and our cats are here.
We will praise God every Sabbath day,
And we will worship our Lord together as
we kneel and reverently pray.

We are growing old together, two become as one.
Soon we will die and then awake to realize our life has only begun.
When we see the form of Jesus coming through the sky
Then we will hear Him say "well done My children,"
And know we'll never more die.
Then we'll here Him say, "well done My children,"
And know we'll never more die.

You bring me so much joy and laughter, Meaning for my life.
How I praise our Lord for giving you to be my wife.

© Rob Simmons. 14.08.2006.

TOGETHER!

Together, it seems so little time.
I still recall as yesterday when you said you'd be mine.

Together, we made ourselves a home.
The children have all come and gone and we are left alone,

But we're together,
And together we have always been.
Together we have made each other strong.
Even if we'd had a hundred years
I'd want a hundred more to come along

Together, when trouble would appear,
We'd pray for guidance from above and
know that God would hear.

Together, we will ever be.
I still don't really understand just what you see in me,

But we're together,
And together we will always be.
Together as we start each day anew,
The greatest wish that's in my heart is to tell
you once again… I LOVE YOU!

© Rob Simmons.

YA LYUBLYU TEBYA!

One day while we were walking my darling sang to me.
My heart was overflowing with the sweetest melody.

My love is like a flower. My darling like a bird.
I'll sing of her forever the loveliest song e'er heard.

Sometimes when there are problems and life is hard to bare,
These words serve to remind us we don't need to despair.

Our love is but a shadow of God's love full and free.
He showed it on Golgotha by dying on the tree.

He showed Ya lyublyu tebya. Ya lyublyu tebya.
Ya lyublyu tebya. I love you. I love you. I love you.

© Rob Simmons.

JERRID.

How fast you're growing now my son, my son.
Soon you will be a child no more.
What will you be when you're a man my son?
What does the future have in store?

Or will you live to only please yourself?
Will you from Jesus turn away?
Will this life mean to you more than Him?
Son you must have the final say.

So soon you will become a man my son.
So soon your life will be your own.
I know that we will still be proud of you
Some day when you are fully grown.

Will you give your heart to Jesus?
Will you love Him as your Friend?
Will you help Him rescue those in sin,
So that this life on Earth will end?
Will you always have the courage
You will need if you're to stay
Faithful to the One Who died for you?
My son there is no better way.
My son there is no better way.

© Rob Simmons.

HAPPINESS.

We loved each other once and we were happy, you and I.
Somehow we had forgotten that, as the years went by.
We used to spend our time together, sharing all we had.
So tell me what has happened dear? When did our love turn bad?

If I am not the most important person in your life,
Who are you dressing up for? Who pleases you, my wife?
Why do you find more pleasure in the friends you meet each day?
And when your money is all gone you then want me to pay.

I have tried through all our marriage to provide for you.
I've worked my fingers to the bone to make you happy too.
So now that we are comfortable and have a lovely home,
We're like two strangers living here and I feel so alone.

I don't care about your money, or the clothes you wear.
I care not about your size or how you wear your hair.
And when I'm working it's your choice of what you want to do.
But when we are at home together dear I just want you.

Love is all I've ever wanted, love is what I need.
As we loved so long ago and could again indeed.
Make me first choice in your life as I will do for you.
Then we'll find the happiness that you and I once knew.

© [Rob Simmons. 06/06/2021.]

GOLDEN BALL.

Golden ball of energy living life so cheerfully,
For Jesus is her loving Savior and He wants to show He cares
Though the world is filled with sadness
Cara's heart is full of gladness,
For whenever there's a problem Jesus always will be there.

When she goes to Sabbath school Cara loves to sing and tell about
The One Who is her greatest hope, on Whom she can depend,
First He made her, then He saved her. Soon
He's coming back to take her
To be with Him in His Father's house. He'll always be her Friend.

Blessed Jesus, walk beside her now and guide her every day.
Please show her how to love you Lord, and teach her how to pray?

Golden ball of energy, living life so cheerfully,
For Jesus is Cara's dear Savior, and Heaven is her home.
With her mom and dad beside her and her angel there to guide her
She can face the day with courage for she'll never be alone.

© Rob Simmons.

MARITUAL BLISS.

The cat's away and I'm a mouse squeak, squeak.
The cat's away and I'm a mouse squeak, squeak.
When the cat's away I come out to play.
I can do what I please and I don't have to pay.
The cat's away and I'm a mouse squeak, squeak.

In my home I know who is the boss.
In my home I know who is the boss.
When at the end of the day I sit down to relax,
And the little lady says, "get of me clean slacks."
In my home I know who is the boss.

I know the children love their dear old dad.
I know the children love their dear old dad.
When at the end of the week I come home with me pay,
And the kids crowd around in a funny sort of way.
I know the children love their dear old dad.

The cat's away and I'm a mouse squeak, squeak.
The cat's away and I'm a mouse squeak, squeak.
When the cat's away I come out to play.
I can do what I please and I don't have to pay.
The cat's away and I'm a mouse squeak, squeak.
I'll nibble at my cheese all day. Squeak, squeak.

© Rob Simmons.

AMRYN GUY.

When you came into the family a helpless little child,
You were like a gift from Heaven, so pure and undefiled.
And by the look of love in your mother's eyes
She's forgotten all the pain.
And I knew for you she'd do it all again.

Son I wonder what your future holds? I wonder what will be?
Will you learn to live for Jesus? I guess we soon will see.
And will you trust in Him for what e'er may come
Whether happy times or strife?
Will you let Him be the One to guide your life?

Amryn Guy, how you love to make us smile.
With your laughing face and your funny looks,
You make life so worthwhile.
And though at times you get into mischief still,

You bring us so much joy.
Amryn Guy our laughing baby boy,
You bring us so much joy.
You bring us so much joy.

© Rob Simmons.

BONITA.

Bonnie is so very pretty, so friendly too you see,
With her big brown eyes and golden hair she looks so fine to me.
Bonnie dearly loves her daddy and she loves to hear me pray,
And I want to keep her with me every single day.

Bonnie loves her little sister so she always shares her toys.
When she goes with her to Sabbath School
they don't make any noise.
Bonnie loves to sing about Jesus and she loves to kneel and pray,
And I want to keep her with me every single day.

Bonnie loves to laugh! Bonnie loves to smile.
Bonnie is a girl who has lots of style.
Bonnie loves to sing! Bonnie loves to play,
And I want to keep her every day.
And I want to keep her every day.
And I want to keep her with me every day.

© Rob Simmons.

TALITHA.

Who is my pretty girl? Who can she be?
Who has the cutest face for all to see?
Who loves to laugh a lot? Who loves to play?
Who loves to see her dad? Talitha Gae!

Who loves the Bible? Who loves to sing?
Songs of the Savior, Jesus, our King.
Who loves her Sabbath School? Who loves to pray?
My lovely daughter, Talitha Gae.

She's my Talitha, God's gift to me.
No matter where she is, with her I'll be.
And when I am feeling down she makes me glad.
I always thank the Lord that I'm her dad.

She's my Talitha, God's gift to me.
No matter where we live with her I'll be.
And when she is feeling sad I'll make her glad.
I thank the Lord above that I'm her dad

© Rob Simmons.

VOETSEK YOU!

I went home to see my wife with amorous intent.
The sun had disappeared and now the evening was far spent.
That she would welcome me with open arms and smile I knew.
Imagine my astonishment when she said voetsek you.

I tried to paint the bedroom but we had a little row.
"You are taking far too long" she told me, "do it now!"
The colour that I chose was red, she said she wanted black.
I only had one thing to say, and that was "you voetsek."

Voetsek you means "get away, and trouble me no more."
Not a friendly thing to say to someone, that's for sure.
It's a term that shows annoyance for a little while.
How much better is a kiss, a hug or just a smile?

Soon my Lord and Savior will return to claim His own.
He will give to each a crown, a harp and golden throne.
He will never tell me "voetsek, get away from Me."
Peace and harmony will reign for all eternity.

© Rob Simmons. 16.6.2006.

THE LOVE OF A FRIEND.

Now what is more precious than silver or gold?
It cannot be stolen or purchased or sold,
And once it is given will never grow old?
The free given love of a friend.

A friend is a person who understands you.
A friend will accept you whatever you do.
No matter what happens he'll help see it through.
How lovely to have such a friend.

Oh Lord, such a friendship is strong, full of zeal,
Dependable, constant however you feel.
Such friendship from you is a gift that is real,
For You are the greatest of Friends.

We have a true Friend in Christ Jesus we know,
For we have been told in His word it is so.
No matter what others may say we will grow
In loving our Heavenly Friend.
In loving our Heavenly Friend.

© Rob Simmons.

DEAR LITTLE JESUS.

Come little children, see the Baby lying
There in a manger. Can you hear Him crying?
Dear little Jesus, Son of God on Earth
He will make the whole world happy for His birth.

Can you see the shepherds come to see Him now?
Can you see the wise men low before Him bow?
Bringing gifts for Him, gold; frankincense and myrrh.
Lovely baby Jesus doesn't even stir.

Dear little Jesus, Mary's baby boy,
How He makes us happy, fills our hearts with joy.

© Rob Simmons.

THE LOVE'S STILL THERE.

LOVING HEART.

The moment of a lifetime, the day she'll long remember
When the seed of love has grown into full bloom.
She stands before her loved one in the presence of her Maker.
The lovely bride has come to join her groom.

In the pulpit stands the preacher,
Come to join their lives together.
"Do you take this man?" she hears the Pastor say.
"Be faithful to each other each
And ask the Lord to guide you,
For a whole new life begins for you today."

And a loving heart is a tender plant to be nurtured every day.
And the more it's loved the stronger it will grow.
Then through all the joys and all the pain
that the years ahead may bring,
The love's still there that's all it needs to know.
The love's still there that's all it needs to know.

© Rob Simmons. 31.12.2001.

PRAYER AND PRAISE.

AT YOUR BIRTH.

Lord Jesus how You loved us! How much You sacrificed,
To come and live among the ones You knew would take Your life.
You could have stayed in Heaven. You didn't have to try,
But You loved us far too much to let us die.

You gave up all Your riches to live in poverty.
Born to bring some hope to those enslaved in misery.
So few were there to honour the helpless Infant King
They didn't know the love that You would bring.

Your birth place was a stable.
A manger was Your bed.
On a pillow made of straw You laid Your head.
The animals around You were the ones to see Your birth.
The King of kings a helpless Babe on Earth,
At Your birth.

© Rob Simmons.

ROCK OF SALVATION.

Jesus, You are the Lamb, and Jesus, You are the Son of man.
Emanuel and El Shaddai Lord, the ever present I Am.
Jesus, You are the King, and Jesus; You are the Lord of life.
No matter how You are called my Lord,
You are ever my Friend.

Jesus, You gave me life. You sent your Spirit to teach me Lord.
And soon forever I'll live with You when You come back again.
So give me strength for today to live and work for You while I can.
Give me courage to serve you Lord, to be a fisher of men.

You're my Rock of salvation Lord.
I'm Yours my whole life through.
You gave Yourself to redeem me Lord,
Now I belong to You.

© Rob Simmons.

OH, GOD OF ISRAEL.

Lord, why do I suffer oppression and pain? I
put forth much effort to make little gain.
I wonder at times if it's all worth the strain,
but you are still with me my God.

Lord, you made the heavens, the land and the
sea, so why do these trials I face trouble me?
You made all your creatures to live and be
free. How great is Your mercy my God.

Mighty Father of Abraham, from
slavery You set Israel free.
Take my slavery to sin away? Oh
Father, please deliver me.

Lord finish in me now the work You've begun.
Prepare me for battle, the race to be run,
'Till I see Messiah, the long promised
One, forever be with me my God.
Oh, God of Israel, mighty in strength and power,
Oh, God of Israel, be with me every hour.

© Rob Simmons.

I'M YOURS LORD.

In the beginning, You fashioned and You made
me with complete freedom to choose,
How to live, whether to love You or rebel, to win or lose.
Lord, sometimes my burdens seem so great, yet still
I love You, and though You slay me I will say,
I am Yours Lord, submissive; quiet and still. I
am Yours Lord, to use me as You will.
If my pain can bring You glory or my pleasure brings You joy,
However You will use me Lord, I'm Yours.

You're the Messiah. You gave Your life to save
me from myself- my foolish pride.
How You loved. They nailed Your body
to the cross the day you died.
Lord, how could I murmur or complain? Help me
to trust You and let You live in me again.
I am Yours Lord, submissive; quiet and still. I
am Yours Lord, to use me as You will.
If my pain can bring You glory or my pleasure brings You joy,
However You will use me Lord, I'm Yours.

© Rob Simmons.

RESURRECTION MORN.

Make me like a sheep Oh Lord that I might follow Thee?
Give me patience to trust You Lord that I may faithful be?
Then when my life is over, my time on Earth is done,
In patient trust I'll wait for Thee to call me safely Home.

Help me Lord to work for Thee while time still lingers on?
Give me courage to live for Thee when others think I'm wrong.
For I know the time is coming when working time will end.
I want others to come with me to meet my dearest Friend.

You're my God. You're my King.
I know that I can trust You with everything.
Then when I shall here that trumpet sound
and time shall be no more,
I'll praise you on that Resurrection Morn, on
Resurrection Morn. On Resurrection Morn.

© Rob Simmons.

THANK YOU FATHER.

Thank You Father for Your love. Thank You for Your peace.
Thank You that you cared enough to make my troubles cease.
And thank You for accepting me just the way I am.
And thank You for the greatest Gift ever given man.

Thank You Father for my friends. Thank You for my home.
Thank You that You're always there everywhere I roam.
And thank You for the family that you've given me.
And thank You that Your only Son died on Calvary.

Thank You Father for Your Word. Thank You I can pray.
Thank You that the Holy Ghost hears every word I say.
And thank You Lord that very soon Jesus will be here
And thank You I can tell my friends He is very near.

I thank You Lord! I praise You Lord!
I serve You Lord! I love You Lord!
I love You Lord! I love You Lord!

© Rob Simmons.

JESUS, OH JESUS!

Jesus, Oh Jesus my Savior and Friend,
Master, Redeemer, the Beginning and End,
You made the sea and land and the Heavens up above.
You made the flowers and man and filled him with Your love.

Jesus, Oh Jesus, in the garden You placed a tree.
A test for man You made it to try his loyalty.
"The fruit," You said, "Don't eat it, for only death results from sin."
He did, so now the Savior's redemption plans begin.

Jesus, Oh Jesus Lord, what have we done?
We've all turned against you though You're Jehovah's Son.
Satan had us conquered and bound in heavy chains.
You gave Your life a ransom to set us free again.

Jesus, lovely Jesus Lord, how wonderful is Your name.
Mighty Prince Emmanuel for all ages You're the same.
You were Michael the Archangel, but You took the form of man.
You came to Earth just to bring us eternal life again.

Jesus, Oh Jesus, how You love us all.
You are always guiding though oft' times we fall.
We're sorry that we caused You so much suffering on the tree.
You died and rose in victory to set all mankind free.
You died and rose in victory to set all mankind free.

© Rob Simmons.

I HONOUR YOU.

You loved me! You gave me life.
Though I rebelled against You, You still want me.
You loved me! Became a Man.
To make me whole it cost You divinity.

I thank You Lord! I praise You Lord!
I love You Lord! I worship You.
I want You Lord! I need You Lord I honour You
For all time. For all time.

You loved me! You died for me.
You gave Your life so I could live with You.
You loved me! You live again.
You're coming soon to give me a life that's new.

I thank You Lord! I praise You Lord!
I love You Lord! I worship You.
I want You Lord! I need You Lord I honour You
For all time. For all time.

You loved me! I'm waiting Lord.
The time for Your return is very near.
You loved me! You gave me power
To testify of You for all to hear.

I thank You Lord! I praise You Lord!
I love You Lord! I worship You.
I want You Lord! I need You Lord I honour You
For all time. For all time. FOR ALL TIME!

© Rob Simmons.

LORD, MAKE US ONE.

You are my brother beloved of the Son, the
Father and Spirit. The three are one.
Born to be part of a great brotherhood, chosen,
predestined to all that is good.

You are my sister, come share these with me, the
emblems of sacrifice, there are but three.
To teach and remind us in Christ we are one, a
part of God's Kingdom already begun.

"This bread is My body. Come, eat," Jesus said. "This
cup is My blood which for you I have shed.
With water for cleansing I purify you and fit
you for service in all that you do."

"This one commandment I ask you to do,
love one another as I have loved you.
Teach and encourage, uphold and forgive. By
this will all men know that in you I live."

Lord, make us one as You are one. One
with You Father, Spirit and Son.
As we partake of these emblems of love, Lord,
make us one. Lord, make us one.

© Rob Simmons.

TRIUNE GOD!

Father God, Creator and Sustainer of all things,
    You gave us life with everything that brings.
        We love You, obey You.

Savior God, Forever one with people You have made
    Our dearest Friend. Now we are not afraid
        To love You, to praise You.

Spirit God, Our Comforter and Teacher in the Word,
    You give us power to share the truths we've heard
        With a friend, with all men.

We who love You give You praise, weak and sinful though we be.
    You Who number all our days offer us eternity.

You are Father, You are Savior, You are Comforter and Friend.
    You are One in Three and Three in One,
        the Beginning and the end.
    You are Alpha and Omega, Self-existent for all time.
    You're our Lord and God and Teacher, You're Divine.

© Rob Simmons. 7.6.2003.

LIFESTYLE.
I'M FAT!

I'm fat! I know it. I really ought to loose weight.
That food surely does taste delicious. Can I have another plate?

I' m fat! Can't help it. No matter how hard I try,
I can't seem to loose any blubber. Why did I eat that cream pie?

I'm fat! Must loose it. It's robbing me of my wealth.
My heart can not handle the pressure. I have poor quality health.

I'm fat! Must change it. I want to see eighty-three.
I'm going to transform my diet. It really is up to me.

God spoke to me through the Bible one day,
He said He wants to live in me.
My body is the temple of the Spirit.
His home for all eternity.

I'm fat! I'm changing. God motivates me for Him.
I need to do more exercising. See ya, I'm off to the gym.

WHO'S FAT? It's working. I've lost forty kilos for sure.
Through exercise and healthy diet, I soon won't be fat any more.
Through exercise and healthy diet…

© Rob SimmonS. 24.5.2002.

NO THANKS!

I went to a party to see friends I knew.
When I arrived they had had a few.
They said, "have a drink" what could I do? This is what I said.

No thanks! I don't drink any more. I'm sick
and tired of throwing up on the floor.
To just wake up without a hangover is so much better to me.

Because of drink a man lost his mind. Each
day he'd only had a little wine.
The nursing home said he's doing fine. He can't remember much.

No thanks! I don't drink anymore. I threw
all my alcohol out the door.
Now I have money where once I was
poor. It makes a lovely change.

I heard a crash just the other day. A baby
girl was killed or so they say.
The drunken fool just walked away. I hope they give him life.

No thanks! I don't drink any more. I want
to stay on the right side of the law.
I don't want to walk through a divvy van's
door. I want to travel safely.

Alcohol will only pickle your brain. Alcohol
can really cause you pain.
Alcohol will only send you broke. It's a pathetic joke.

A man went home really drunk one night.
He and his wife had a terrible fight.
He hit her so hard she ran away in fright,
and has never been seen again.

No thanks! I don't drink any more. I've finally
found someone worth living for.
My wife and my Lord whom I adore deserve much better from me.

© Rob. Simmons. 22.1.99.

TESTIMONIES.

I am a prophet.
All through the countryside I roam,
Without a place to call my home.
Though many come to hear me when I 'rise to speak,
To tell God's message to the mighty and the meek,
So few believe enough to turn from doing wrong,
But still I must speak on.
I know they don't have very long

I'm a disciple.
I follow Jesus through the land.
I am a member of His band.
I see Him heal the sick; the leper and the blind.
To those with troubled hearts He brings them peace of mind.
Although they crucified Him on Golgotha hill,
Yet He is living still.
He has fulfilled the Father's will.

I am a martyr.
For faith in Jesus Christ I died, just as my Lord was crucified.
I'm resting now but soon I'll hear the trumpet sound,
Then with the ransomed host for Heaven I'll be bound,
To live in happiness a life that will not end.
I will be with my Friend.
On Him I always will depend.

I am a preacher.
I call the people to the Lord, The Holy One to be adored.
I glorify His name in sermons all my days.
I magnify Him to all men in songs of praise.
I'll see the Holy One from Heaven soon descend.
My joy will never end.
For I will praise His name again and again and again.

© Rob Simmons.

WHERE IS LOVE?

When I look into my future I don't like what I see.
Lonely nights and empty days are looking back at me.
How can life have meaning without someone to care?
What is there to hope for when there's nothing but despair?
Where is love? Where is love?

I had a 'phone call from a friend. I told her how I feel.
She gave to me some good advice to help my heart to heal.
"Forget about the future, it's worry and dismay.
The future will care for itself, so live your life today.
Live today, Live today."

Now it seems the more time passes the stronger I will be.
People who were once so cold are friendly now to me.
The companionship I'm finding is helping me to learn,
The more that I give love away the more it will return
From my friends. From my friends.

The future holds no terror now, I live from day to day.
The love of those around me means much more than I can say.
But the thing that makes me stronger is when I understand,
Jesus walks beside me now and leads me by my hand.
He is love. He is love.

© Rob Simmons.

I QUIT!

When I was about fifteen I recall someone saying to me,
Come and have a puff on my cigarette and see what fun it can be?
So I had a puff and I tried to inhale,
But I started to gasp, I was feeling kind of pale.
Then I cried out with an awful wail,
"That's it! I've had enough! I quit!!!!"

Well somehow or other I didn't you know
'cause I lit up a smoke again.
And now it's been twenty years or more
and I'm feeling a lot of pain.
My lungs are so black they make coal look pale,
And I know that my health is beginning to fail,
'cause it hurts every time I try to inhale.
"That's it! I've had enough! I quit!!!!"

Well this time I did and it sure feels great
to be able to breathe again.
I can taste my food and the cough's nearly
gone and I haven't got so much pain.
Now I've learned some things and I know for sure,
If I hadn't started smoking I wouldn't be so poor.
I thank the Lord that I can say it once more,
"That's it! I've had enough! I quit!!!!"
"That's it! I've had enough! I quit!!!!"
"That's it! I've had enough! I quit!!!!"

LITTLE GIRL.

Little girl sitting in family worship listens to her mother say
"Always read your Bible dear, and don't forget to pray."
"I will always love You Lord!" says the little girl in her heart.
"I will never let You down nor from Your ways depart."

Many years pass and the lovely little girl has now turned seventeen.
Getting home late from a date one night, her
mother asks her where she's been.
"Leave me alone!" screams a pretty young
lady with rebellion in her heart.
"Got to get away," she is saying to herself
"got to make a brand new start."

Now the young lady has joined her lover
but she still has found no peace.
Trying to forget the pain of a guilty conscience that will not cease.
She is searching for a way to have some peace of mind.
Fills her body with drugs from a needle that her lover had left behind.

Groaning and crying from the drugs she's taken,
her body now wracked with pain.
She remembers her family and wishes that
she could become a child again.
"Help me God, please help me now and I'll come back to You.
You're the only One who has the power to see me through."

Pain now passing and she thanks the Lord
for her life and for her health.
Now she sees that her faith in God is by far her greatest wealth.
God had always loved her even when she had run wild.
Now she's sure that her Father in Heaven
still wants her to be His child.
Now she's sure that her Father in Heaven
still wants her to be His child.

© Rob Simmons.

PATIENT'S LAMENT!

Come lend an ear you people here
and listen while I prattle.
I have to take so many pills that when I walk I rattle.
And the doctors that I see have all become quite wealthy.
It costs a fortune just for me to stay a little healthy.

I went to see my doctor and he told me, "you are sick."
You've got to hand it to my doctor, he is very quick.
"Just to be sure with some specialists I must confer.
But with my diagnosis I am sure they will concur."

He saw…
A Cardiologist, a Haemotologist, an
Ophthomologist, an Endocrinologist,
A Rheumatologist, a Gastroenterologist, a Proctologist….
and a G.P.

Now there's pain and suffering as a normal part of life,
And it seems there's nothing anyone can do.
but the Master didn't make me to remain a broken man.
He promised He will soon make all things new.

Soon now the Great Physician will be coming to the Earth.
To gather all His people for a wonderful rebirth.
Then there will be no sin or sickness, suffering or pain,
All trace of sin will disappear when Jesus comes again.

There'll be…
No Cardiologist, no Haemotologist, no
Ophthomologist, no Endocrinologist,
No Gynaecologist, no Gastroenterologist, no Proctologist....
and no G.P.

HOPE

I ASKED THE LORD.

I asked the Lord for freedom, freedom from all the pain.
Freedom from all discouragement, freedom to serve again.

I asked the Lord for comfort, comfort that's in His Word.
Comfort that comes from knowing, knowing that God has heard.

Jesus is living freedom, freedom and peace and love,
Comfort and hope eternal, free from My Lord above.

He said, "My child, abide in Me,
Then all these things are thine.
Go now. Be strong. Tell everyone
These are My gifts divine."

© Rob Simmons.

JUBILEE SABBATH!

When I think about the Sabbath day, and what it means to me,
Of the fellowship I have with my spiritual family,
And how I worship You as Creator Lord, and Redeemer of my life,
With my loved ones there, my children and my wife,
Through Your Son and through Your Spirit
Lord, You made a man your child
Then You placed him in a garden so pure and undefiled.
Oh how I long to be in that garden Lord,
where I never more will stray.
How I long for that Eternal Sabbath day.

Father God, You are Creator of all things.
You're the centre of the Sabbath day, and all the joy that it brings.
And as I rest from daily labour Lord, I find my strength in You.
Through Your Word You show me what is true.
I give my life to You.

© Rob Simmons.

BLESSED SABBATH DAY.

In six days You made creation, animals and flowers and man.
But the seventh day You rested. Blessed Sabbath day began.

Six days are for work You've told us. Time for us to try our best.
But the seventh day is holy. Blessed Sabbath day of rest.

On the Sabbath we can worship, pray and read Your Word anew.
Teach and serve our friends and others,
showing love as You would do.

Holy day! Happy day! Day that celebrates creation.
Lovely day! Precious day! Blessed Sabbath day of rest.

© Rob Simmons.

COME OUT!

John in Revelations saw three angels flying high.
Three final messages the Lord did send.
They filled the earth with glory, their trumpets sounding loud
To prepare us for the very end.

The first angel has sounded out his call to serve the Lord.
"Fear God and give Him glory" was his cry.
His righteous robe your covering, your vindication sure,
For your Redeemer quickly draweth nigh.

The gold of faith and love is found in Jesus Christ alone;
The only gold of value to the Lord.
Love the truth He's given and love your fellow man.
Worship God and live forevermore.

"You must worship Me alone" is what the Lord commands.
"All other gods will only bring you pain.
Babylon is fallen so partake not of her sins.
For Babylon will never rise again."

Here's a call for wisdom, let the people turn to God.
The eye salve of the Lord is needed now.
The third angel is sounding, let his words be understood.
And let the Spirit come to show us how.

Worship not the Beast. His image you must not obey.
God is bringing evil to an end.
The Devil and his counterfeits will soon be swept away
When Jesus takes us to the Promised land
Come out of her My people, why join the living dead?
I'll see you through the trials just ahead.
Come out of her My people, partake not of her plagues
Accept my sacrifice and you'll be saved.

© Rob Simmons.

NIGHT TIME PRAYER.

Jesus knew that the time was short. There was so much to be done.
So many still in ignorance, so many to be won.
But He felt so tired from His heavy load
and He knew that He must rest.
Now the day was done and the night had come.
It was time to be refreshed.
It was time to be refreshed.

He had worked so hard through the heat of the
day and in the freezing cold of night,
He had nowhere to lay His head, no shelter was in sight.
So He went down on His knees in prayer
and to His Father said at length,
For the day to come and the work to be done
Oh Father, give Me strength.
Oh Father, give Me strength.

Then He looked around. The night was nearly done.
He'd meet the throngs of people with the early morning sun.
He'd heal their sick and dying; the halt; the lame; the blind;
He'd forgive people of their sins and bring them peace of mind.
He'd bring them peace of mind.

Now He's met with God and His mind's at
peace, refreshed now for the day.
He can see the people coming, they need to know the way
To the path that leads to Heaven, of that better land to come.
Now He works so hard in the heat of the day
In the hope of saving some.
In the hope of saving some.

© Rob Simmons.

GIANTS!

Twelve men were sent by Moses to spy out the land.
How those grapes could grow so big they couldn't understand.
The figs were big as cantaloupes, all produce ripe and fare.
In the land of milk and honey there was abundance everywhere.

But the land was filled with giants, a fierce and savage foe.
Ten spies said, "We cannot beat them, we might as well just go."
But two men said, "trust in the Lord and He will win the fight.
He promised us possession here and He will do what's right."

So put your faith in practice. Lend a helping hand.
Share this story with your friends. Help them to understand,
That when they face their giants of sin or doubt or fear.
The Lord is mighty. He can make those giants disappear.
Some think that they can enter in with great effort applied.
But the best we do is full of greed and selfishness and pride
We cannot earn salvation. That's already been done.
It's a gift that's freely given us by Gods' beloved Son.
A land of milk and honey is waiting for us now.
It's not hard to enter there. Our Savior showed us how.
Love the Lord with all your hearts and love your fellow man.
Follow His commandments, through Jesus Christ you can.

So put your faith in practice and lend a helping hand.
Share the Gospel with your friends. Help them to understand,
That Jesus really loves them and soon He will be here.
Eternity begins right now. There's nothing more to fear.

© Rob Simmons. ©20.11.2001.

IN VERITY!

God has given guidance to His people today.
Council that confirms His Word, illuminates our way.
Given to prepare a people for the Earth's last hour,
Giving us the strength to stand, through the Spirit's power.
They are both the same. The council to the Laodiceans
Is the third angels message in verity.

To the Laodiceans was wise council given,
To deliver us from sin, to prepare us for Heaven.
Faith and love and understanding, righteousness in Jesus,
Purchased without cost or money, given to redeem us.
They are both the same. The council to the Laodiceans
Is the third angels message in verity.

Worship not the Beast, his image we must not obey.
Trust the Lord with all our hearts, to Him only pray.
All the wisdom of the world will only bring us pain.
Jesus Christ will give true life when He comes again.
They are both the same. The council to the Laodiceans
Is the third angels message in verity.

Listen now my people, hear the mighty Midnight Cry.
Jesus Christ will soon be here. Can't we even try
To warn the people of their state? Invite them to the Savior
Where alone they have the hope of life in Him forever.
They are both the same. The council to the Laodiceans
Is the third angels message in verity.

Jesus is calling. How will we reply?
They are both the same. The council to the Laodiceans
Is the third angels message in verity.

© Rob Simmons. 22.12.2002.
Based on Revelation 3:18,19; & 14:11,12.

GOODBYE!

Now it's over, it's time to sleep. I've lived
my life for God, now it's His to keep.
The day will come when I'll rise again
with body new and free from pain.

I have trusted in Christ alone to be my Guide
through life, and to lead me home.
At death's approach I will trust Him still
to keep me safe within His will.

All the trials I've faced through life, and all
the pain I've known, all the tears and strife
Won't matter, when I see Jesus smile. That's
when I'll know it was all worthwhile.

Time has come now for me to die. For
just a little while in the grave I'll lie.
Soon I must pass through death's dark
doors. Yet will I live forevermore?
Yes! I will live forevermore.

© Rob Simmons. 15/08/2006.

SHAMA YISRAEL.

Listen, Shama Yisrael.
The Lord our God, the Lord is One. The Lord our God is One.
Adonai, Elohiyno, Adonai, echad.
The Lord our God, the Lord is One. The Lord our God is One.

[Deuteronomy 6:4.]

Yea, though I walk through the valley of the shadow of death,
I will fear no evil.
For thy rod and thy staff, they comfort me,
and I will dwell in the house of the Lord forever,
I will dwell in the house of the Lord.

[Psalm 23:4, 6.]

I will extol Thee, my God, O King;
And I will bless Thy name for ever and ever.
Every day will I bless Thee; and I will praise Thy name
For ever and ever.

[Psalm 145:1, 2.]

Listen; shama Yisrael.
The Lord our God, the Lord is One. The Lord our God is One.
Adonai; Elohiyno; Adonai; echad.
The Lord our God, the Lord is One. The Lord our God is One.

© Rob Simmons. 14/03/2021.

WORDS!

I wrote a song to praise the Lord, in church I sang my song.
It had three verses and a bridge, it wasn't very long.
I sang my song with heart and voice to praise my God, my King,
'Till someone told me afterwards I don't know how to sing.
So I don't sing there now.

I played guitar to praise my Lord, I played it for my Friend.
I played in church, I played the songs with gusto to the end.
It felt so right to worship God with soul and string and song.,
'Till someone told me afterwards my playing was all wrong.
So I don't play there now.

The thing I have to ask myself is why I sing and play.
It's not for praise; it's not for fame; and surely not for pay.
If there is one who reads my poems or hears the words I sing
Can chatch a glimpse of my best Friend and all the joy He brings,
I'll share my poems now.

My God has shown me many ways to serve and work for Him.
So if I really want to serve my Savior Elohim,
I will ignore the words of some, and do the best I can
To sing and play for God so someone may be led to Him
I'll use my gifts for Him.

© Rob Simmons. 22/05/2021.

DO AS YOU'RE TOLD!

All your life you've been a rebel. All your life you've been so wild.
By living far from the ways of God, your life was so defiled.
Do as you're told!

Now you want to be a Christian. Now you want to be at peace.
You want the pain of the past to go so you're mind will be at ease.
Do as you're told!

Still the devil wants to keep you, so he binds you to you're sins.
He knows he'll lose his control of you when
your life with Christ begins.
Do as you're told!

When you know the Lord is calling, when you hear Him speak to you,
When the Holy Ghost whispers in your
ears and He tells you what to do.
Do as you're told!

Many people will you gather, many people will you win,
When you let the Lord have control of you,
when you give your life to Him.
Do as you're told!

© Rob Simmons.

FACE IN THE WAVES.

As I went walking down by the seaside, I
saw a Face in the waves of the sea.
The Face I saw there I held so precious; the Face of Jesus my Lord.

Sometimes, in trouble, I get discouraged. One
set of footprints in the sand I would see.
I'd cry "oh Jesus, why don't you help me?"
Those prints were His, He carried me.

Jesus was there in the waves of the sea. Jesus
was there on the sand close by me.
With Jesus by my side I knew I was free.
The Face in the waves of the sea.

JESUS DIED FOR ME.

Now some people say that I'm not right in the head,
And there are times that I think that I'd be better off dead.
Still I seem to recall that in the Bible I've read
That Jesus died for me.

Now maybe they're right that I'm a little bit slow.
And there must be a lot of things that I 'm yet to know,
Still slowly but surely I'm starting to grow,
'Cause Jesus died for me.

I don't care if some think that I'm not worth very much,
For I do know my Father and He doesn't think such.
Now I'm being made perfect by the Masters touch,
'Cause Jesus died for me.

Yes my Jesus died when He came to this Earth,
But He wouldn't die for junk, so I must be of worth.
Now I'm free to rejoice that mother gave me birth
'Cause Jesus died for me.

Yes, my Jesus died when He hung on the cross,
And though it cost all He had so that I wouldn't be lost.
He freely gave up His life. He took my sin and my dross,
When my Jesus died for me.

BORN AGAIN!

[Baptism.]

I went to the water for to be baptised, to wash my sins away.
When I rose from the water I knew I was
clean 'cause I'd been Born Again.

When I went to the water for to be baptised
the Holy Ghost was there.
He gave me His power so that from that day Jesus I could declare.

Now I've been with Jesus for so many
years. On Him I must depend,
For I know that the Devil wants to tear me
down but I've been born again.

Born again! Born again! Born of the water and the Spirit.
Born again! Born again! I know that it's Heaven I'll inherit.

© Rob Simmons.

THIS IS MY BELOVED SON.

[GOD THE SON.]

Jesus knew that the time had come to leave his mothers' home.
For three and half-short years all through
the country He would roam.
Then He went to the river Jordan, where of John He was
baptized.
A carpenter no longer, now Messiah, the Christ.
With water streaming down His face His ministry begins.
He longs to touch the people and to free them from their sins.
Then the Holy Ghost came on Him in the fashion of a bird.
With a mighty sound like thunder, the Father's voice was heard,

Simon Peter and James and John were with Him on the way.
He told them where He'd go and where He wanted them to stay.
Then they watched Him climb the mountain,
high above the Jordan's plain.
In a brilliant flash of light they saw their Master had changed.
His face and clothes were shining bright,
His hair was white as wool.
To see their Lord transfigured was for them so wonderful.
Then as Moses and Elijah spoke to Him they looked the same.
From the sky the Father's message could be heard again.
When He said...

This is My beloved Son in whom I am well pleased.
This is My beloved Son to Him you must pay head.
I have given Him to you now just to show to show you who I am,
And how you can find Me again.

© Rob Simmons.

REVELATIONS 3.

I asked my Lord when He is coming and
    why His coming seems so slow?
He said, "My people, you're still not ready.
    Like little children you need to grow."
He said, "My people, you're still not ready.
    Like little children you need to grow."

I asked my Lord, where is His Spirit? We
    badly need His latter shower.
He said, "My children, you're so indifferent.
    My Holy Spirit can't use you now."
He said, "My children, you're so indifferent.
    My Holy Spirit can't use you now."

My God said, "Christian, you must obey Me
    and you must follow where e'er I lead.
Now go buy gold that's been tried in fire for
    faith and love is the gold you need."
"Now go buy gold that's been tried in fire for
    faith and love is the gold you need."

My Lord said, "people, you need white raiment.
    You need these clothes to be right with Me.
And you need eye salve My special ointment
    so that the truth you may clearly see.
And you need eye salve My special ointment
    so that the truth you may clearly see."

I asked my Lord would He forgive us? Would
He forgive our lukewarm state?
He said, "My children, I've won the battle.
There are so many still ruled by hate.
Please tell your neighbor's how much I love them
and help Me save them from Satan's fate.

© Rob Simmons.

I'M FREE!

Once I thought that I had all I wanted in this world.
I thought that I knew everything, that I was in control.
I didn't know I was a slave held fast by all my sins.
But now I've met with Jesus Christ made He made me whole again,

Jesus tried to help me but my progress was so slow.
He led me just as quickly as my stumbling feet would go.
So patiently He waited 'till I chose to let Him in,
And then He took away from me my stubborn bent to sin,

Jesus raised me high from the world of sin,
And He showed me what life could be.
He has healed the scars sin had left on me,
And He caused my eyes to see, Now I'm free! I am free!

Jesus said to gather all the people I could find.
He told me I'm to bring them in, the halt, the lame, the blind.
He wants to heal their bodies and their minds in every way.
Together then, rejoicing, they with me can truly say,

That now I'm free! Praise God I'm free!
I have been set free! Jesus has control now over me.
Jesus has control over me.

© Rob Simmons.

I ASKED MY WAY.

I asked my way to Heaven, here's what was said to me,
"Go feed your hungry brother." That's what was said to me.
"For if you feed your brother you will be feeding Me,
Then you will eat from My table." That's what was said to me.

I asked my way to Heaven, here's what was said to me,
"Give water to the thirsty." That's what was said to me.
"By giving water to others you're giving water to me.
Then you can drink from My fountain."
That's what was said to me.

I asked my way to Heaven, here's what was said to me,
"Go welcome in the stranger." That's what was said to me.
"For if you welcome the stranger you will be welcoming Me.
Then you will live in My kingdom." That's what was said to me.

I asked my way to Heaven, here's what was said to me,
"Go now and clothe the naked." That's what was said to me.
For if you clothe the naked then you'll be clothing Me
And I will give you a robe pure white." That's what was said to me.

I asked my way to Heaven, here's what was said to me,
"Go visit those in prison." That's what was said to me.
"For if you visit the prisoner then you'll be visiting Me.
In safety you'll walk on streets of gold."
That's what was said to me.

I asked my way to Heaven. Here's what was said to me,
"Good works alone won't save you." That's what was said to me.
"By ministering unto others you are becoming like Me.
Then I will give you a crown of life." That's what was said to me.

© Rob Simmons.

HE SAID, "MY CHILD..."

God can You help me? how do I handle this? What should I do?
Lord, how do I cope with rejection, when
those whom I love turn on me?
Their slander and malicious gossip, cause
me great heartache and grief.
Lord, soon I must face unemployment, when
my place of work, closes down.
Then what will I do for a living? It seems there is nothing a round.
Lord, how can | bare all this sorrow? I
think, of the hours I've cried.
Please tell me Lord why I'm still living, now
my dearest loved one has died?
He said, "My child, I feel your pain.
But if you trust Me, I will make everything work for your good."
He said, "My child, I gave My Son to die in agony
So you might live with me forever.

© Rob Simmons.

SATAN, YOU'RE A LIAR.

"Come on over to the right side," Jesus said to me.
"Leave your sin and your rebellion, I can set you free.
I alone can give salvation. I alone can take your pain.
If you follow and obey Me, in my love you will remain."

"Come on over to the dark side," Satan said to me.
"Life with me can be a party, live it wild and free.
You can be the greatest lover. You can dance and smoke and drink.
Lose your fears and inhibitions. Do whatever you can think."

I don't want to be a lover. That could break my heart.
I don't want to be a drinker. Drugs I will not start.
All that Satan has to offer quickly loses it's appeal.
I choose Jesus and salvation. He's the only one Who's real.
Jesus, I will follow you. Satan, you're a liar.
Lord, you give eternal life; Satan death by fire.

© Rob Simmons

JESUS, CITY OF REFUGE.

In Israel there were many cities into which people could run.
When, being guilty of manslaughter, a deed accidentally done.
They were to be cities of refuge where people could find a home.
Escaping the anger of others they could live in peace alone.

In Jesus there is found a city of refuge from guilt and shame.
To forgive men for their transgressions, now that's the reason He came.
They have need to only confess them,
forsaking what brought them grief,
Then willingly serving their Savior they'll find true peace and relief.

Jesus is a city of refuge for all those who from sin will turn,
Who want to become more like Jesus, who
willingly from Him will learn.
But those to whom sin is more precious then following in Jesus' way
Will suffer the full consequences of rebellion on Judgment day.

Be my City of Refuge. Save me from the guilt of my sin.
Give me Lord a heart to obey and Your Spirit within.
Jesus You're my City of Refuge.
Jesus You have purged me from sin.
You forgave and cleansed me that I may a new life begin.
You forgave and cleansed me that I may a new life begin.

© Rob Simmons. 27.2.01.

IT'S NOT ENOUGH!

When Moses was about forty years old
he knew God's rules for sure.
But the Lord couldn't use him 'cause he killed a
man so he had to wait forty years more,
Till at last he came to understand that God must rule in his heart.
Only then could he keep God's rules and lead
his people to a brand new start.

Now Saul was a man who kept the law as well as any man could,
But he didn't have that peace of heart the way he knew he should,
Till he met the Man the law spoke about
on Damascus road one day.
There the Lord told Paul where he was to go
and what He wanted him to say.

Well even now when we go to church we can still hear people say
If you want to get to Heaven you've got to
obey God's rules in every way.
We can only pray they'll come to see that life with God is free.
It's the gift He gives so they can live with Him for all of eternity.

It's not enough to know the rules of God.
It's not enough to know the rules of God.
It's not enough to know the rules of God.
You've got to know the God of the rules.

HE IS!

You say that God's just imagination?
You say that He isn't real, but you're wrong.
You say that we just evolved from the sea?
Come over here. Carefully listen to me!

Who made the grass? Who gives life to the flowers?
Why do we live? Who can have such great power?
Who made the stars? Who controls what they do?
That takes someone with more power than you.

Why can't you see that **He is** and that He made you and me?
What must He do just to prove how much He really loves you?

He proved His love when He hung on a tree.
He proved His power when from death He broke free.
He proved that He really meant what He said,
When He said He'd wake us up from the dead.

Now that you know that the Savior is real,
And that He does understand how you feel,
Why don't you let Him come in to your life,
And free your soul of its sin and its strife.

Why can't you see that **He is** and that He made you and me?
What must He do just to prove how much He really loves you?
Just to prove how much He really loves you?
Just to prove how much He really loves you?

© Rob Simmons.

WILL YOU BE THERE?

For so many years we've been hearing the story told,
That Jesus Christ is coming back some day.
We've heard about the signs in the heavens and on the Earth,
But now we see it happen just that way.

It's written in the heavens and it's written on the Earth,
It's written in the songs that children hum,
That soon the graves will open when the trumpet call is heard.
Will you be there to see the Savior come?

Soon death and persecution will be coming to our land.
Our trials here it seems have just begun.
Through faith and love for Jesus we'll with courage make a stand,
Then with the saints we'll shine forth like the sun.

It's written in the heavens and it's written on the Earth,
It's written in the songs that children hum,
That soon the graves will open when the trumpet call is heard.
Will you be there to see the Savior come?

The trouble times are starting, things are getting really bad.
At times it seems that you're the only one.
So many apostatizing, they're leaving the faith of God,
But now we see so many new ones come.

It's written in the heavens and it's written on the Earth,
It's written in the songs that children hum,
That soon the graves will open when the trumpet call is heard.
Will you be there to see the Savior come?

That small dark cloud is growing over in the eastern sky,
Soon sin and sorrow will be swept away.
Our Savior now is coming. Sons of Adam, shout for joy.
Rejoice and sing, this is Salvation Day.

It's written in the heavens and it's written on the Earth,
It's written in the songs that children hum,
That soon the graves will open when the trumpet call is heard.
Will you be there to see the Savior come?

© Rob Simmons.

QUESTIONS!

I had so many questions. Things I wanted to know.
What is truth? What's important? What can stay? What must go?
Then I heard one say to me, "there are some things for real,
You and God and this planet, how does that make you feel?

Then I asked him a question, what does God want of me?
I know I am a sinner. Death is sins penalty.
Jesus died to redeem me. Paid the debt that I owe.
I know I don't deserve it that he could love me so.

Now I know I'm a Christian. Now I know what I am.
I have hope for the future. I have Jesus my Friend.
Help me Lord to show other that they like you may grow.
With the ransomed forever I'll be living I know.

God has made you and He loves you.
This world exists by His power.
And He wants you just to love Him,
Be His each and every hour."
Be His each and every hour."

© Rob Simmons.

REDEMPTION!

Many stories that are told, sermons couched in language bold,
Tells how Christ will come again, thus to put an end to pain.
Men and women saved from sin will eternal life begin.

But there is another story, tells of those not found in Glory.
People who were not prepared. Here them
cry? See how they're scared?
All their lives chances were given that
they may prepare for Heaven.

Now they see the Lord appear. Too late now His voice they hear.
Evil people shout in vain; curse, blaspheming Jesus' name.
Crying for some rocky place, "fall and hide me from His face."

Thus the evil people die. On their lips a curse, a cry.
Yet, some faithful, just a few, bodies changing, all is new.
Gazing now into the sky, know that they no more will die.

Hear these people how they pray. "Come to Me" they hear Him say.
"A place I have prepared for you. Mansions there and gardens too.
In My land there is no sin. Now eternal life begin.
Now eternal life begin."

© Rob Simmons.

RUN TO JESUS!

All of my life I'm fighting a battle, tempted
to sin, which way will I go?
Will I let Satan's lying deceive me, or run
to the only shelter I know?
Sometimes I think I'm stronger than Satan, that
he cannot harm me or tempt me to sin.
Quickly I find my strength is illusion, for
every time the Devil would win
Now that I know that Satan is stronger, that in
my own strength I have no power at all.
My only hope is in running to Jesus. By
trusting in Him I never will fall.
Only Jesus has conquered sin. Only Jesus was strong.
Only Jesus can help me choose to turn and flee from all wrong.
Willingly I give my life to Jesus, I give to
Him my mind, body and heart.
I long to see Him coming in Glory, then
Jesus and I we never will part.
Run, run, run, run! Run straight to Jesus, flee from temptation.
Run, run, run, run! Jesus alone can keep you from wrong.

© Rob Simmons.

WE HAVE SEEN HIS STAR!

Come let us go to Israel now for we have seen His star.
Prepare the food and camels now, our journey will be far.

To Herod came the wise men asking,
"Where's the Jewish King?
We've traveled over many miles that we may worship Him."

To Bethlehem the wise men went and said to Joseph, "Sir,
Please may we give to Him our gifts of
gold frankincense and myrrh."

They humbly gave to Him their gifts then joyfully went their way.
Today the Christians of the world can also truly say,

That we have seen His star now yes we have seen His star.
We know the Savior has been born for we have seen His star.

For we have seen His star now yes we have seen His star.
The Savior now reigns within our lives for we have seen His star.

© Rob Simmons.

STRANGE FIRE!

Nadab and Abihu were both priests before the Lord,
Serving in the temple night and day.
Burning fire and incense with the offerings they received,
But their sinful hearts were far away.

Cloven tongues of fire fell upon the faithful few,
Giving them the Holy Spirits power.
But another spirit came to those who disbelieved,
Like a burning fire to devour.

Many in the church today are living for the Lord.
Many have another spirits fire.
If they don't repent the Lord will surely visit them.
In the burning flames they will expire.

Lord, I want to give to You my body and my heart.
Lord I want to be Your child today.
Very soon the time will come for Jesus to return,
Then strange fire will be far away.

Strange fire; offered in the temple.
Strange fire; death was there reward.
So carelessly they mocked the Lord,
But He could not accept strange fire.

Strange fire; take it from my heart Lord,
Strange fire; keep it from my mind.
I want to be Your child today,
And be delivered from strange fire.

© Rob Simmons.

MATTHEW 23.

One night, on a hill, Jesus stood alone.
So many times He tried to change their hearts of stone
In that city.
It was only time, He knew it had to pass, the temple made
of stone could not receive the love He had given.
The temple is the heart where God alone should dwell.
How could even God their sickness heal.
He would not use force, all He could do was plead.
How can it be they're so slow to believe?
It's up to them to see their need.

"Jerusalem," He sighed, "My pleading soon will end.
Where then will you turn? There is no
other friend who will help you.
Fools, why is it so? Why must you be so blind?
You follow all the rules, but love I cannot find.
You're so empty."
Tears came to His eyes, the visions that He saw.
The people brought their troubles on themselves.
They didn't want His love. They killed the ones before.
By His rejection they have doomed themselves.
Now they must pay for Calvary.

"Hypocrites!" He cried. "To you I cast the blame,
You Pharisees and Scribes, to Me you're all the same,
Those that hate Me.
Many men will die as they turn from My love.
Because of all your lies, they're cut off from above, From My city.
To Moses' law you cling, but it won't help you now.
You've forgotten what it's all about.
You can hardly see what Moses knew so well;
There's only one way mankind can be free.
That way is me through Calvary."

They crucified my Savior. They hung Him high on a tree.
I wonder if to the Savior we'd do the same thing today?

One night, on a hill, Jesus stood alone.
He wept for all the ones who just would not be told
Of His love.

© Rob Simmons.

OUR WONDERFUL GOD.

Oh, what a marvelous promise is given,
That God will supply every need,
When in our lives we give to God first position.
The Lord in His love has decreed.

God is the Architect. He is the Builder,
Of all that on this planet is.
Our bodies, our time and our every possession,
Are on loan to us, but they're His.

The cattle which graze on the hillside are Gods.
To Him everything does belong.
For we are but stewards and not the true owners.
To think otherwise would be wrong.

For all of His kindness and wonderful caring,
He asks but a small thing you know,
That willingly we give our tithes and our offerings.
Our love for Him thereby we show.

Oh, what a blessing to us has been promised,
If only faithful we would be,
In bringing our offerings and tithes to the storehouse.
Then God's blessings we would receive.

© Rob Simmons.

PEOPLE

WOMAN AT THE WELL!
[JOHN 4.]

The day was hot. I had to drink. The water was all gone.
The others had rejected me, still I had to be strong.
Alone I traveled to the well. Alone I stooped to draw.
My bucket full, I paused to rest to drink and thirst once more.

I heard a voice. A Man had asked, "will you give Me to drink?"
Who was the man? A hated Jew. I had to stop and think. "Why
do You ask this thing?" I said. "We have no dealings Sir,
For You're a Jew and I'm a woman of Samaria."

"Come drink from the water I offer you and you will thirst no more.
The gift of the Father I give to you, the love you hunger for,
For I am the water of life indeed, the Father's only Son.
You wont find salvation in someone else for I'm the only One."

"To have this gift, there is one thing that I want you to do.
Your husband I want you to find and bring him here with you."
"I have no husband Sir." I said. "I know," was His reply.
"Though five you've had you live in sin. In this you do not lie.

"Come drink from the water I offer you and you will thirst no more.
The gift of the Father I give to you, the love you hunger for,
For I am the water of life indeed, the Father's only Son.
You wont find salvation in someone else for I'm the only One."

In awe I rushed into the town as fast as I could run.
"Come see a Man who told me all the things that I have done.
The Holy One is here and we're to worship God through Him.
No longer in Samaria or in Jerusalem."

"Come drink from the water I offer you and you will thirst no more.
The gift of the Father I give to you, the love you hunger for,
For I am the water of life indeed, the Father's only Son.
You wont find salvation in someone else for I'm the only One."

© Rob Simmons.

THEY BROUGHT A WOMAN TO JESUS.

They brought a woman to Jesus to see what He'd do with her.
They caught her in the act of adultery. The
law said she should be stoned.
They asked the Teacher, "what do You say?
The law says she should be stoned.
You teach forgiveness and love for man. The
law says she should be stoned.
But tell us Teacher, what is Your plan? The
law says she should be stoned."

Jesus looked at them and He started writing in the sand.
He said, "He without sin cast the first stone."
As one poised to throw He would write his sin on the ground until
He and the woman were left alone.

He said to the woman, "now, look around. How many do you see?"
She lifted her eyes up from the ground.
"Why Master, they've gone away."
"Woman, I want you to be My child. I have saved you from the law.
It hurts Me to know that you're running wild.
Now go away and sin no more.

They brought a woman to Jesus to see what He'd do with her.
To see what He'd do with her. To see what He'd do with her.

© Robsimmons

HE LIVES

[THE PASSION OF CHRIST.]

On Friday He hung on the cross bleeding and dying in pain.
The soldiers, the people and priests mocked and derided His name.

On Sabbath He lay in the tomb in safety where none could molest.
Now having completed His task the King of the world lay in rest.

On Sunday the tomb was laid bare. The angel had shifted the stone.
In triumph He'd risen again for all of my sins to atone.

Now Jesus the conquering King is waiting His ransomed to claim.
And soon with the angels of God forever I'll proclaim His name.

> Now I know that my Savior lives.
> Now I know that He's free.
> He lives in my heart and directs my ways.
> He's everything to me.

© Rob Simmons.

70 X 7.

Peter started boasting about the way he'd grown.
He told about the seven times forgiveness he had shown.
But You told him that was not the way You wanted Him to live.
Then he asked You Lord how many times
did You want him to forgive?

When I think of Peter it still amazes me
How he forgave the ones who hated him so bitterly.
But seventy times seven was only just the start.
You wanted your forgiveness to completely fill his heart.

Jesus, in Your churches we are Peters living still.
We sing about how much we love but don't obey Your will.
Lord, show us how to live now and take away our sin?
Remind us Lord of Peter and the words you said to him.

When You said, "Seventy times seven." Lord, how can it be?
You said, "seventy times seven," but that's much too hard for me.
Still You always have forgiven me and made me whole again,
So help me Lord forgive and love my fellow man.

© Rob Simmons.

THE BIBLE COMES ALIVE.

When Moses led his people out to cross the desert sand,
Then Pharaoh's army tried to take them back to Egypt land.
God opened up the waters so that Israel could go through,
But Egypt drowned when they thought they could too.

When I read how David killed Goliath with a sling and stone,
Of the fish that showed poor Jonah where God wanted him to go,
Or the time God shut the lions' mouths so Daniel could survive,
That's when for me, the Bible comes alive.

When I pray to the Lord and I open His Word,
Then for me the Bible comes alive.
That's when for me the Bible comes alive.

© Rob Simmons. ©1986.

MARTHA!

Lord I've been working so hard all day
to make these loves of bread,
And the other food You see here to get Your disciples fed.
But all Mary does for hours is sit here listening to You.
If I don't get some help soon I don't know what I'm gonna do.
What am I to do?

Lord the kitchen's a disaster and the lounge room is a mess,
But until the house is tidy Lord You know that I can't rest.
All the dishes must be washed and all the rubbish must be gone,
All the carpets must be tidy and all things where they belong.
Lord, is that so wrong?

Lord You know I tend to worry over things both big and small,
But I only want to do my best, to give to You my all.
Help me know how to submit to You and
leave things in Your hands.
Show me how to serve You better Lord, please help me understand.
Let me know Your plan?

Martha! Martha! Thou art trouble and vexed over many things,
But only one thing is needful, and Mary has found that good part,
And it won't be taken from her.
No I'll never leave you My dear children.

© Rob Simmons.

I DON'T HAVE TO LEARN JAPANESE.

I have to go to work all day and do my best to earn my pay,
But there's one thing I'm glad to say, that
I don't have to learn Japanese.

Now only healthy food I buy like vegetables and bread of rye
So I don't get too fat and die, but I don't have to learn Japanese.

I love to sing and play guitar and I could really be a star
Who's name is known both near and far,
but I don't have to learn Japanese.

Once every week we kneel and pray to welcome in the Sabbath day
And praise our Lord in every way, but I
don't have to learn Japanese.

At last this poem's nearly done. The first
draught lost, this second one
Has been a work of love begun, but I still haven't learned Japanese.

I may enjoy the Iron Chef, or write my songs with treble cleft,
But I will never feel bereft if I don't have to learn Japanese….

Unless I want too.

SAYENARA!

© Rob Simmons.

ODE TO FATBUM!

She was just a cat.
She was small, and black, and bent.
She was just a cat.
Nobody would want her nor give her a home.
She was just a cat.
Not very friendly, hissing at most.
She was just a cat.
Demanding and smelly and fussy
She was just a cat.
But she was God's gift to us.
She was just a cat.
But for we who loved her, she was our baby, our joy.
She was just a cat.
But she had her way of showing kitty love.
She was just a cat.
But she was warm, and soft, and trusting.
She loved to cuddle and purr and headbutt.
She was just a cat.
But for 14 years she enriched our home, our hearts and our lives.
Yes, just a cat.
But she will be sadly missed.

© Rob Simmons. 17/05/2014.

THE CAT!

I am the cat. God made me that. Been
sleeping all day, sleep my life away.
I don't have a worry, a trouble or care. Whenever
I need them, my people are there.
I am **the CAT!**

I love to eat all kinds of meat from a silver tray, it tastes better that way.
And when I am done I jump on the lap of one
of my people, and then take a nap.
I am **the CAT!**

I'm a cool cat! I'm a crazy kitty! I'm a spoiled cat,
And I love it and want it to stay like that.
I am **the CAT!**
I love to purr and lick my fur. I'll pounce on
a mouse or a moth in the house.
When I go outside I really have fun, I'll play
with a cricket or laze in the sun.
I am **the CAT!**

I **am** the cat, I **am** the cat, *I* am the cat, I **am** the cat,
I **am** a pretty, real cool kitty,
I **am** the cat, I **am** the cat, I **am** the cat, I **am** the cat,
I'm a cool cat! I'm a lucky cat!
I'm a black cat! Who called me fat?
I AM THE CAT!

www.ingramcontent.com/pod-product-compliance
Lightning Source LLC
LaVergne TN
LVHW011826060526
838200LV00053B/3912